DAVID BELASCO

Naturalism in the American Theatre

LISE-LONE MARKER

# *David Belasco*
## Naturalism in the American Theatre

PRINCETON UNIVERSITY PRESS

Library of Congress Cataloging in Publication Data
will be found on the last printed page of this book

Publication of this book has been aided by a grant from
the WHITNEY DARROW PUBLICATION RESERVE FUND of
Princeton University Press

Composed in Linotype Granjon and printed
in the UNITED STATES OF AMERICA by
Princeton University Press
Princeton, New Jersey

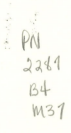

*For* FRED

# Contents

vii

CONTENTS

# Illustrations

ix

Photographs are reproduced through the courtesy of the following institutions: Theatre and Music Collection, Museum of the City of New York (Figs. 5, 10, 11); Theatre Collection, New York Public Library (Figs. 6, 7, 8, 9); University of Toronto Library (Fig. 3); and the Yale Theatrical Prints Collection (Fig. 4).

# Foreword

GENERALLY REGARDED AS ONE of the first significant directorial figures in the history of the American theatre and dutifully named in every survey work together with such pioneers of stage naturalism as André Antoine and Constantin Stanislavski, David Belasco has, paradoxically, received none of the critical attention accorded his celebrated European counterparts. Associated as a director neither with a Chekhov nor an Ibsen nor a Strindberg, Belasco's exuberant theatricality has come to be regarded with prim suspicion by critics concerned mainly with the purely literary aspects of drama. This book, like its flamboyant subject, is not for them. Its aim is to provide, for the first time, a stylistic analysis of the scenic art of one of the American theatre's most fascinating practitioners. Its "bias" is that the significance of his historical role in the rise of stage naturalism demands balanced reevaluation.

In surveying a career that spans six decades from its beginning in San Francisco in 1871 to Belasco's death in 1931, no chronological parade of his many productions would prove effective or even readable. Instead, an attempt has been made to synthesize the aims, methods, and techniques inherent in the naturalistic production style which Belasco evolved. The elements of that style—the magic reality of his stage settings, his innovations in plastic lighting, his directorial method—are also seen in terms of the influence of theatrical developments elsewhere. On the basis of this synthesis four of his most important productions, each representative of a distinct phase of his directorial art, are then reconstructed and explored in greater detail.

Contemporary newspaper and periodical criticism has frequently proved extremely helpful in recapturing the flavor and tissue of Belasco's performances. By allowing these contemporary viewers, particularly William Winter, to speak with their own voices on occasion, something of the social and cultural texture of the times emerges as well.

Much more important, however, are the previously untreated primary sources upon which this study has so fortunately been able to rely. The George Pierce Baker Collection of the Yale School of Drama Library, the Harvard Theatre Collection, and particularly the Museum of the City of New York, with its collection of Belasco promptbooks and photographs, have all yielded valuable information. By far the richest mine of facts about Belasco's productions is, however, the Theatre Collection of the New York Public Library, originally founded for the purpose of housing the David Belasco papers. Their holdings comprise an impressive selection of Belasco's promptbooks and typescripts, a variety of scene photographs, press cuttings, memorabilia, and other contemporary documents which provide the scholar with a secure foundation upon which to reconstruct Belasco's production style in the light of theatrical history.

I am indebted to the officials of all these institutions for their continued kindness and cooperation. In particular, I am grateful for the help and courtesy extended to me by the late Sam Pearce and by Mary Merrill of the Museum of the City of New York, by Paul Myers of the New York Public Library Theatre Collection, and by Mary Grahn, former librarian of the Yale School of Drama. Among those who have given this study the benefit of their advice and friendly criticism during the various phases of its preparation, I am especially conscious of my debt to the late Professor Torben Krogh, sometime Professor of Theatrical History at the University of Copenhagen, and to Professor A. M. Nagler of Yale. Less directly but no less perceptibly, I have derived inspiration from the characteristic kindness of the late Alan S. Downer of Princeton, to whose work every historian of the American theatre feels a debt. For a memorable afternoon filled with pleasurable reminiscences of "Mr. B," I am grateful to the late Mrs. Burk Symon, widow of Belasco's stage manager. To Jo Mielziner, I owe a special debt of gratitude for the encouragement which his kind interest has given me. On the editorial side, I am indebted to R. Miriam Brokaw, Associate Director and Editor of Princeton University Press, and to Margot Cutter, for their patience and assistance in guiding this study through the various stages from script to book.

A Research Fellowship from the University of Copenhagen supported and encouraged my early research in Belasco and the American theatre. A Humanities Research grant from the University of Toronto aided me in the preparation of the present manuscript for publication. The book has been published with the help of a grant from the Whitney Darrow Publication Reserve Fund of Princeton University Press.

Above all, my deepest gratitude and warmest appreciation belong to my husband, Frederick J. Marker, to whom this book is dedicated, and to whose own extensive knowledge, unfailing encouragement, and enthusiastic help and guidance it owes more than I could ever hope to express.

LISE-LONE MARKER

Toronto
*January, 1974*

# DAVID BELASCO

Naturalism in the American Theatre

# Legend's End

*It must be borne in mind that methods
and fashions on the stage are variable
and that the theatre always reflects the
taste and proclivities of its own time.*

DAVID BELASCO

FEW MEN have influenced the American theatre as decisively as David Belasco, and none has been as methodically
maligned for his pains. Adherents of the so-called New
Stagecraft in the twenties, while drawing upon many of
the very methods and innovations of Belasco, conveniently
attained the cohesiveness necessary for any revolution by
ascribing to him all the collective faults of the naturalistic
form they rejected. The critical spokesmen for the militant
new movement were, as spokesmen for militant new
movements often are, witty, urbane, determined.

"It goes without saying that Mr. Belasco has no supreme
gift of any sort," proclaimed Stark Young, adding the observation which, to the stark new generation of seekers
after "dramatic truth," would appear most damaging:
"Events, people, passions, the arts, his private and personal
experience, his joys and sorrows he can see in only one
light; without footlights, in sum, without footlights he
is blind."[1] The sarcasm of George Jean Nathan, in an
article entitled "Legend's End," was more devastating and
therefore less susceptible to rebuttal. To make his point

3

that Belasco "has worked a vast and thorough ill to the American playhouse and its drama," Nathan trained his scathing wit on the renowned "studio" of "the Belasco," where "with much flourish and ado, much subtle greasing and tony flim-flam, the newspaper theatrical writers" were occasionally invited (never, mind you, Nathan himself). "A single wax taper, inserted artistically in a Limoges seidel, illumined the chamber with its ecclesiastic glow," this critic recorded, "and in that [glow] was glimpsed a single narcissus in a wistful pot. Upon the inlaid onyx commode that served as a desk rested carelessly a framed photograph of Dante, with the inscription 'To my warm friend, Dave, in token of his services in the cause of art'— and duly autographed by the poet in that peculiar and unmistakable flowing hand of his."[2]

Today, of course, the charm of Belasco's deep-dyed theatricality suggested by these statements (themselves now so distinctly "of a period") draws a smile. But revolutions have notoriously little patience with either "charm" or "historical influences." Moreover, the legend of the Bishop of Broadway carefully and methodically disseminated by critics of the twenties such as Stark Young and Nathan has been perpetuated in subsequent, generally cursory, evaluations of Belasco, obscuring his contributions to the theatre and the nature of his scenic art. Perhaps no legend is ever without some foundation of truth. Yet to achieve a reliable evaluation in historical terms of Belasco's production style, the legend I have been describing must be laid aside. In doing so, this book endeavors to function as a reappraisal.

Belasco's own observation that the theatre always reflects the taste and proclivities of its own time is particularly appropriate to his own productions. These reflect in a variety of ways the style and tastes prevalent in the American theatre at the close of the nineteenth and the beginning of the twentieth century. Although Belasco must be said to be America's principal exponent of naturalism in the theatre, his treatment of the naturalistic aims and tenets has never been analyzed at length in the perspective of theatrical history.

In fact, David Belasco's productions should be viewed against the background of the conventions and techniques of stage naturalism: ensemble playing, detailed psychological motivations and objectives, realistic stage atmosphere, and, first and foremost, directorial autocracy. Some elements of Belasco's production style contrast sharply with Continental interpretations of naturalism, while others have direct European parallels. Each of Antoine's aims—the perfection of scenic illusion, the elimination of footlights and painted canvas, the creation of an acting ensemble in which the players moved *among* the furniture and substituted significant business for grandiloquent acting—was shared by Belasco. His scenic style was, in addition, characterized in all its phases by a strongly accentuated theatrical intensity, recalling in many ways the romantic period and its use of intense emotional expression in the theatre. Yet Belasco's basic coordination of individual details into an harmonic ensemble places him among the outstanding exponents of naturalism. When the Moscow Art Theatre visited New York in 1923, it was no coincidence that critics found that the Russian style of production had nothing new to teach Broadway; following the visit Stanislavski seemed to explain this fact by making Belasco an honorary member of the M.A.T.

5

During nearly half a century of association with the New York theatre, David Belasco was involved with no fewer than 123 Broadway productions. He directed ninety-five plays and produced (in some cases directing as well) seventy-two. In all, thirty-four of his own plays and adaptations were performed on the New York stage, and during his remarkable career Belasco had a hand in the authorship of nearly two hundred plays in all. The plays which Belasco produced were chosen or written by him with a keen sense of the practical theatre as his guide. His repertoire cannot be called remarkable for its purely literary value. But his passion for artistic unity and perfection and his capacity for uncompromising labor to attain these goals made him one of the most influential men in the history of the American theatre. "In most things that concern bringing a drama to life on the stage," wrote Walter Prichard Eaton in a perceptive article published four years after Belasco's death in 1931, "he was a pioneer and perfecter; he taught our crude theatre the lesson of detailed discipline; he brought to it mood and atmosphere and sensuous beauty; above all he showed us that to achieve a final effectiveness one guiding intelligence must rule a theatre. He taught us how to unify the diversified arts of the modern playhouse and make them one art."[3]

It is to the genesis and composition of that art that this study now turns.

## CHAPTER ONE

# *Beginnings*

DAVID BELASCO arrived in New York City, then as now the theatrical heart of the United States, in 1882. Within a short time he had established a reputation as the nation's foremost naturalistic director and, subsequently, as a producer of international renown. The beginning of Belasco's Broadway career in 1882 marked more than simply a significant personal milestone. Changes were taking place at this time which affected world theatre profoundly; stage naturalism was waging a decisive struggle again the older, established theatrical conventions and practices.

In 1881, one year before Belasco reached New York, Zola published his celebrated essay collection, *Le Naturalisme au théâtre*. This manifesto and the earlier preface to his play, *Thérèse Raquin* (1873), exposed "the decayed scaffoldings of the drama of yesterday" and defined a new goal for the theatre, designed to bring it "into closer relation with the great movement toward truth and experimental science which has, since the last century, been on the increase in every manifestation of the human intellect." "There should," Zola went on to proclaim, "no

7

longer be any school, no more formulas, no standards of any sort; there is only life itself, an immense field where each may study and create as he likes. . . . We must look to the future, and the future will have to do with human problems studied in the framework of reality."[1]

For Zola, as for Edmond de Goncourt who in the foreword added to *Henriette Maréchal* in 1879 characterized the theatre of his time as "cette boîte de convention, cette machine de carton," the world of the stage had become a cardboard world of artificial contraptions having nothing in common with observed reality. The new movement called for a complete rebirth of the theatre, replacing stagnation and rigidity with something vital and alive, "giving a shiver of life to the painted trees, letting in through the backcloth the great, free air of reality." Zola, and later André Antoine, around whom the scenic realization of the naturalistic concepts in France came to revolve following his sensational directorial début in 1887, were not blind to the fact that all theatre builds upon convention, including the convention of "naturalness." A barrier always exists between the fictive theatrical world and the real one. The aim of the naturalistic theatre man, however, is to reduce that barrier to a minimum and to increase realistic authenticity to a maximum. The essence of the naturalist's endeavor was an objective, scientific exploration of reality that rejected all readymade formulas and conventions. He should, insisted Zola, attempt to represent on stage "a fragment of existence," or, as the critic-playwright Jean Jullien phrased it, "a slice of life."

To this idea of verisimilitude Zola added another important principle: the concept of environment as a conditioning element and a reality to be reckoned with, or changed, by the individual. The purpose of the realistic, true-to-life stage setting is to make the characters in the drama more real to the audience by placing them in their proper milieu. In dramatizing *Thérèse Raquin*, wrote Zola, "I tried continually to bring my setting into perfect accord with the occupations of my characters, in order that they might not *play*, but rather *live*, before the audience."[2] Hence the set was counted upon to concretize the vital role played by environment in the dynamics of existence. Antoine emphasized that he in fact found it indispensable to create the proper milieu for a production before preceding further with the *mise-en-scène*. "For it is the environment that determines the movements of the characters, not the movements of the characters that determine the environment. This simple sentence," he continues, "does not seem to express anything new; yet that is the whole secret of the impression of newness which came from the initial efforts of the *Théâtre Libre*."[3]

The notion of the stage as an environment in which the characters live a life of their own became a fundamental tenet of the theatre of the late nineteenth century. We encounter this concept with increasing frequency both in Europe and America from the 1880s on. It expressed, as John Gassner succinctly observes, "a sturdy allegiance to reality as the middle-class civilization of the late nineteenth century conceived it to be." It provided a reality "of human beings feeling and acting in places and with objects around them about which there could be no mistake: the characters were specifically located and specifically occupied with material realities in a material world."[4] A realistic décor was no mere pictorial accompaniment to the action of a play. It acquired individual

9

character and meaning as a determining force capable of undergoing observation and analysis.

Hence the naturalistic director's justification for his meticulous attention to material, outward details—in setting, props, lighting, and so on—was not rooted in a fascination with these things *per se*, but was based on the conviction that the sum of them accounted for or aided in establishing an inner authenticity. The stage setting was relied upon to convey the conditions of life which were the subject of the play. The terms "naturalism" and "realism" have today acquired an imprecise meaning that suggests only the trivializing influence of drabness, externality, and lack of selectivity. Originally, however, naturalism sought to present the facts of man's life and environment with a fresh, new, and rich explicitness. "If dramatic art is anything at all, and if it is worthy of being perpetuated," Belasco emphasized, "the reason is that it is, above everything else—far above the mere purpose of supplying pleasurable entertainment—an interpretative art, which portrays the soul of life." At the same time Belasco felt an obligation to confront his audiences with truth: "the mirror which reflects nature to them in the theatre must be neither concave nor convex. Its illusion must be true, and only to the extent that it is true will it successfully stir their imagination."[5]

In terms of actual theatrical practice, the naturalistic emphasis upon the deterministic role played by each significant, verisimilar detail implied a central guiding principle: the necessary integration of the various elements of play production—setting, lighting, costumes, and acting—in a meaningful, unified whole. In achieving this integration, the figure of the director emerged as a power hitherto unequalled in the theatre. It is through no coincidence that the names associated with the establishment of naturalism are frequently those of directors: André Antoine in France, Otto Brahm in Germany, Constantin Stanislavski in Russia, William Bloch in Scandinavia, and David Belasco in America. In the English-speaking countries the traditional actor-manager was replaced during this period by the figure of the producer-director.

The program for theatrical reform promulgated in Zola's naturalistic credo had the distinct character of a battle cry advocating the establishment of a new style and the overthrow of older traditions. In contrast, those usually credited with the actual realization in practice of the principles of naturalism generally resented narrow, programmatic labels. In his memoirs, *Mes Souvenirs sur le Théâtre Libre*, Antoine emphasizes again and again that his objectives were never narrowly programmatic but were dictated mainly by the desire to create good theatre.[6] Antoine's *Théâtre Libre* was, as its name suggests, designed as a free, experimental theatre liberated from the restricting and outworn classical traditionalism of institutions like the Paris Conservatoire. J. T. Grein's Independent Theatre (1891) and Otto Brahm's *Freie Bühne* (1889) were established on a similar pattern. Brahm's remark, enunciated in his manifesto proclaiming the establishment of "a Free Stage for Modern Life," is typical in this regard: "We are friends of naturalism and we want to go a good stretch of the way with it—but we should not be surprised if, in the course of the journey . . . the road should suddenly turn and astonishing new vistas in art and life should emerge."[7]

The later founding of the Moscow Art Theatre in 1898

was more in the nature of a direct revolution. "We protested," states Stanislavski, "against the customary manner of acting, against theatricality, against bathos, against declamation, against overacting, against the bad manner of production, against the habitual scenery, against the star system which spoiled the ensemble, against the light and farcical repertoire which was being cultivated on the Russian stage at that time." But, admonished the man whose name has become practically synonymous with naturalism in the theatre, "those who think that we sought for naturalism on the stage are mistaken. We never leaned towards such a principle. Always, then as well as now, we sought for inner truth."[8]

In contrast to these contemporary exponents of new theatrical standards, David Belasco's scenic style did not evolve out of any particular spirit of revolt or desire for freedom. Nor was it hailed at the outset, as was the case with Antoine, as a pioneering realization of a new aesthetic program. This fact should not, however, be taken as a sign that Belasco's significance in the practical theatre of his time was thereby of relatively lesser magnitude. Scandinavia's William Bloch, whose revolutionary productions of Ibsen and Holberg at the Danish Royal Theatre have become legendary, likewise evolved his naturalistic style without notable conflicts or clashes with the theatrical tradition in which he found himself.[9] Any thorough investigation of the contribution of Stanislavski or Antoine or Bloch to the living theatre of their time would of necessity concern itself with the stage conditions that existed in their respective countries, in order to show why their efforts were or were not compelled to take the form of a revolt. Similarly, for a proper evaluation, the productions of David Belasco must be viewed in their true perspective, with some knowledge of the environment which nurtured them and the contemporary theatrical taste which accepted them. Although Belasco's importance rests on his achievements in the New York theatre, the early part of his career in California should not be neglected. Basic factors influencing his artistic outlook and attitudes can be traced to his early experiences and impressions from the theatre of the West Coast. Countless articles and interviews, including "My Life's Story," the rather inaccurate account of Belasco's life published in *Hearst's Magazine* from March 1914 to December 1915, provide eloquent testimony to the fascination which this early period held for Belasco. The spirit of romance and extravagant adventure with which the theatre of his youth was imbued continued to manifest itself in subtle ways in his later work, from his selection of dramatic subject matter to the atmosphere which pervaded his productions.

THE ENVIRONMENT in which David Belasco grew up was in itself the stuff of picturesque romance. He was born in San Francisco on July 25, 1853, at the peak of the Gold Rush, of Portuguese Jewish parents who had recently emigrated from England to California and had opened a small shop. When exciting reports of gold in British Columbia touched off a great migration northward in 1858, the Belasco family moved with the stream to Victoria. The highlight of the theatrical season there in 1864 was the appearance of Charles Kean and his wife, on a farewell world tour, in a number of Shakespearean productions. This luminous occasion afforded the eleven-year-old

Belasco his first significant professional engagement, as the young Duke of York in *Richard III*.[10] Legend has it, however, that his actual stage debut occurred several years earlier, when he was "carried on" at the Victoria Theatre Royal as Cora's child in Sheridan's *Pizarro* by the lovely Julia Dean Hayne, who made several tours of the Pacific coast during the 1857-1858 season; apparently Belasco was often utilized for small juvenile parts at this theater.

Early in 1865 the Belasco family made their way back to San Francisco, where David distinguished himself at the Lincoln School through his precocious declamatory abilities, in recitations of such promising pieces as Matthew Gregory Lewis's *The Maniac*, and took his first faltering steps as a dramatist with *Jim Black, or The Regulator's Revenge* and similar efforts now fortunately lost.[11] During these early years the stage-struck Belasco appeared occasionally as a supernumerary at the local theatres, and he succeeded in organizing an amateur theatrical society. Hence he was no stranger to the world of the theatre when he embarked in earnest upon his chosen career in 1871, following graduation from Lincoln School. During the years that followed he worked furiously to establish himself in the theatrical profession, touring up and down the coast with any company that would hire him. He acted parts, served as an extra, copied prompt-books and scripts, "doctored" plays, and gained his first experience as a stage manager under the rigorous and primitive conditions to be encountered "on the road." "Many a time," Belasco told his biographer with relish, "I've marched into town banging a big drum or tooting a cornet. We used to play in any place we could hire or get into—a hall, a big dining room, an empty barn; anywhere! . . . and in that way I got my first experience as a stage manager—which meant being responsible for every-thing."[12] "In all my study of theatrical history," the re-doubtable William Winter noted, "I have not encountered a person more downright daft, more completely saturated in every fibre of his being, with passion for the Stage and things dramatical than was young David Belasco."[13] It was a time to plan and dream, and as Belasco later recalled with satisfaction: "One cannot begin to dream too soon if one expects to transform the dream into reality, and I believe that most men who have accomplished anything have had the dream in early boyhood."[14]

The repertory to which Belasco was exposed during these early years represented a broad and colorful cross-section of nineteenth-century American theatre, ranging as it did from minstrels and burlesque to the plays of Bou-cicault, Bulwer-Lytton, and Shakespeare. His barnstorm-ing ventures as a strolling actor included a wide variety of bigger parts: Uncle Tom, Claude Melnotte in *The Lady of Lyons*, Fagin in a stage version of *Oliver Twist*, Ar-mand Duval in *Camille*, Mercutio, Antony, and even Hamlet. During the years until 1876, when Belasco gained a more permanent foothold in the San Francisco theatre as a stage manager and later as a director and dramatist, he continued to play innumerable bit parts in a generous sampling of the popular melodramas of the nineteenth century. Their titles, legendary as they are, conjure pow-erfully and speak for themselves: *Rip Van Winkle, The Hunchback, London Assurance, The Ticket-of-Leave Man, The Corsican Brothers, The Child of the Regiment, The Marble Heart, Under the Gas-Light, The Two Or-phans, The Rough Diamond*, and many more.[15] Because

Belasco never achieved any particular distinction as an actor, his endeavors in this area are generally regarded merely as a footnote to his subsequent accomplishments in the theatre. These endeavors provided him, however, with an effective introduction to the art of acting generally and to the techniques of some of the greatest actors and actresses of the age: Lawrence Barrett, John McCullough, Walter Montgomery, E. A. Sothern, James O'Neill, and Edwin Booth among the former, Adelaide Neilson, Lotta Crabtree, Charlotte Cushman, and Helena Modjeska on the distaff side. These stars, who illuminated a brilliant, golden era in the American theatre, made an indelible impression on young David Belasco. "There was something in their facial expressions, something in their voices, that thrills me in memory even now," he wrote thirty years later. "It was not, I am sure, because they were the first great actors and actresses that I had seen—it was something in them, something that impressed and would impress us today. You take a woman like Charlotte Cushman. She had what we call the heavy attack . . . she had none of the subtle, refined ways that we desire in our players; but should she play today, you would find that she would impress us just the same as she did the last generation. She might have to change her methods, for the methods are now different, but she was always human in what she did; so she would be human now, and it would be through that humanity that she would reach us."[16]

Such observations by Belasco are noteworthy not only for what they tell us about the much admired art of Charlotte Cushman, but also for the differences they suggest between the style of acting that prevailed in the theatre of Belasco's youth and the changed style in vogue later, dur-

ing the naturalistic period. Belasco's recollections of Edwin
Booth highlight these differences still more clearly. Booth
played an eight-week engagement at the California Theatre in San Francisco during the 1876-1877 season, appearing together with John McCullough in a number of his
most celebrated roles—Hamlet, Richard III, Othello, Bru-
tus, and Richelieu (Bulwer-Lytton). Belasco signed on as
an extra merely in order to be on the stage with the great
actor. "I shall never forget those performances," he recalled. "Booth was my *great* idol. . . . I found him very
uneven—that is, his performances were not always up to
his own standards. But when he was really 'in the vein'
there was *nobody* like him; there never has been, and
there never will be! I never heard such a voice—so full of
fire, feeling, and power—and I never saw such eyes as
Booth's, when he played King Richard the Third, Richelieu, or Iago."[17] The two hallmarks of Booth's acting
which Belasco found remarkable, his voice and his exceedingly expressive eyes, must be understood in the context of a performance tradition which placed maximum
emphasis on elocution, mime, and picturesque, plastic
beauty in stage poses. This method of expressing dramatic
emotion by means of accentuated mime and visual scenic
"attitudes" gradually disappeared with the advent of naturalism in the theatre. The attempt to represent as accurately as possible on the stage the texture of daily behavior
necessarily eliminated all striving for artifice or accentuated effects in the appearance and deportment of the
actor. This evolution took place slowly and by degrees,
however, and the early productions of David Belasco continued to embody numerous inheritances from the older
acting style.

Another key to the style personified by Booth and the other great names in the theatre of Belasco's youth was the preeminent position of the star actor. The principal aim of a production was not to evolve a carefully orchestrated and integrated ensemble in the modern sense, but to present effects created with complete independence by the star. Belasco's recollections of Edwin Booth shed much light on the rehearsal practice underlying such virtuoso productions. "At first I used to go to the California [Theatre] to watch his rehearsals, but I soon found out it was little use," Belasco told Winter. "The plays were all an old story to him and he wouldn't rehearse. McCullough had Booth's promptbooks, and Booth left the company pretty much to him and just 'ran through' the big scenes with the principals."[18] The fact that carefully integrated ensemble effects were neither generally desired nor possible to achieve in the San Francisco theatre of this period is further emphasized by Belasco's observation that less than one week's rehearsal was the norm for preparing a new play for performance.[19] Ensemble playing of the kind desired by the naturalists, in which the director worked closely with each character and then, in the words of the gifted naturalistic director, William Bloch, "assembled the various individualities into a musical harmony of conversation in the inspired life of the ensemble,"[20] presumed a system of rehearsal and performance radically different from that prevailing in the California theatre of Belasco's youth. So long as fewer than seven rehearsals were usually required for a full-length play, and each actor as a consequence remained sovereign in the preparation of his own role, there could be no possibility of achieving the precise scenic teamwork of the entire ensemble which characterized naturalism.

The limited number of rehearsals was an intrinsic factor in the earlier theatrical practice, in accordance with which each actor prepared his part independently and resented or distrusted interference and advice from others. Under these conditions, a director was plainly a superfluity, useful only for informing the players about sets, entrances and exits, handling of props, and positions on stage in crowded scenes requiring more complicated blocking. William Winter, who personally experienced both the era dominated by such independent virtuosi of the stage as Edwin Forrest, Joseph Jefferson, Edwin Booth, and others and the period during which the ideals of coordinated ensemble playing first took form, notably in the productions of the autocratic Augustin Daly, Belasco's immediate directorial predecessor in the New York theatre, definitely considered the older system superior. "A radical error in the stage management of the late Augustin Daly (who was a superb stage director) arose from his propensity to insist that every part should be acted in strict accordance with his personal view of it," Winter warned. "The iron-clad application of this rule . . . would inevitably efface individuality in an actor and convert him into a machine."[21] Winter's opinions concerning the proper areas of function for a director echo an attitude typical of the period before directorial autocracy became predominant in the art of the theatre. "The most essential service that such a functionary can do," the critic asserted, "is to watch the performance from the front; to note its virtues as well as its defects; and, while he suggests rectification of the faults, to cheer his company by intelligent recognition of the merits. The actor . . . should be allowed to express his own ideal of a part—unless that ideal be manifestly and demonstrably wrong—and should not be constrained to fetter and stultify himself by striving to embody the ideal formed by another mind and arbitrarily thrust upon him."[22]

The practical significance of a statement like this had, however, been lost long before it was pronounced (1908), due in no small way to David Belasco's insistence that a single will must reign in the theatre, and a single spirit must permeate and activate the entire production. "The director energizes; he animates. This is what Max Reinhardt understands so well how to do," observed Robert Edmond Jones a decade after Belasco's death. "A curious thing, the animating quality. Stanislavski had it; Belasco had it; Arthur Hopkins has it. One feels it instantly when one meets these men. One sees in them what Melville calls 'the strong, sustained and mystic aspect.' "[23] During his New York period Belasco customarily rehearsed a play which presented no special difficulties for a total of six weeks in order to achieve a suitable ensemble. In so doing he much preferred to train his own stars, utilizing inexperienced, younger actors rather than attempting to adapt the independently minded actors of the old school to his overall interpretation. "In making my dramatic productions I have nearly always found my resources as a director put to a much harder test with actors of long experience, whose manner and method have become fixed in certain definite lines of parts," he remarked, "than with those, perhaps of much more limited technical proficiency, who have not gone beyond the pliable state, when they are still susceptible to new methods of expression."[24] Stanislavski made a similar decision in turning from the older actors "to the young people," teaching his system "to young actors and actresses picked from among the supernumeraries in the [Moscow Art] Theatre and the pupils of the school."[25]

During Belasco's early years in San Francisco, it was obviously impossible for him to create new methods of expression in acting; merely the staggering burden of productions in which he was involved—William Winter's calculations arrive at a figure of 300 in a ten-year period—precluded this.[26] Nevertheless, Belasco's avid interest, evident from the very beginning of his career as a stage manager and performance supervisor, in preparing each production with the utmost discipline and care, and his striking ability to exercise authority over every aspect of a performance plainly foreshadowed his future eminence as America's master of carefully integrated ensemble playing.

When a troupe from A. M. Palmer's renowned Union Square Theatre Company in New York, starring James O'Neill, arrived in San Francisco in the spring of 1878 and Belasco served as their director, his services proved unusually valuable. He was presented with a special bonus of two hundred dollars and a flattering letter of recommendation by the company "for your able direction of our efforts." Belasco's "quick apprehension and remarkable analytical ability in discovering and describing the mental intentions of an author are so superior to anything we have heretofore experienced," the letter continued, "that we feel sure that the position of master dramatic director of the American stage must finally fall on you."[27] In 1876 Belasco had become prompter and assistant stage manager to James A. Herne, and subsequently became stage manager at San Francisco's plush new theatre, Baldwin's Academy of Music. This playhouse was managed by the remarkable theatre magnate Tom Maguire, whose long career (1849-1882) contributed in no small measure to the glamor and color of the California stage. His repertoire ranged from minstrels and musical comedies to legitimate drama, featuring such imported luminaries as Barry Sullivan, Charles Fechter, Adelaide Ristori, and Adelaide Neilson, whose lovely Juliet Belasco always remembered as one of the greatest acting presentations he had ever seen. Belasco kept his position at the Baldwin, with few interruptions, until he left for New York in 1882, functioning not only as director but also accumulating valuable experience as a dramatist and an adapter of plays to fit the company's requirements.

During an acting stint at Piper's Opera House (a happy combination of saloon, playhouse, and gambling den) in Nevada's great boom town, Virginia City, in the fall of 1873, Belasco had served as a secretary to Dion Boucicault, America's most sensational playwright of the seventies. His own statement suggests the benefit he derived from this association, which enabled him to observe the celebrated dramatist's methods at first hand. "There is no doubt that even though he adapted—in accordance with the custom of the time—he added to the original source, making everything he touched distinctly his own," recalled Belasco, much of whose own work would follow the same pattern. "He left everything better than he found it; his pen was often inspired, and in spite of his many traducers, he was the greatest genius of the Theatre at that time. Boucicault was a master craftsman."[28] This evaluation of a playwright whose supreme talent lay in "a felicitous dexterity in making a story tell itself in action rather than in words,"[29] in his spectacular and tremendously popular melodramas, is significant not so much for what it says about Boucicault as for what it tells us about the bent of Belasco's taste, his ceaseless and frequently expressed admiration for craftsmanship in the theatre. The heightened emotionalism, stunning incident, and spectacularly realistic scenic display which were hallmarks of Boucicault's fame also manifested themselves in Belasco's work, particularly during his early San Francisco period. Obviously these elements also typified numerous other productions of this period of stirring scenic spectacle, however, and it is difficult to determine the exact measure of Belasco's debt to the influence of Dion Boucicault. Belasco embarked on his theatrical career at a time when the taste for gaudy display and exciting spectacle in American show business was at its height. This was the age of extravagantly staged melodramas, farces, and romantic plays, the age of equestrian shows, *tableaux vivants*, vaudeville, Negro minstrels, and a great deal else, and also the age of Shakespearean productions with such stars as Booth and Lawrence Barrett, exhibitions of strikingly picturesque scenery enhanced by "atmospheric" and festive music.[30] When performances were announced to the public, the splendor of "new" scenic display was as highly "puffed" as the exciting content of the play and the name and abilities of the leading actor or actress. Hence David Belasco's abiding fascination with theatre remained a fascination with all of these facets combined.

In the spring of 1877 Belasco allied himself, as actor-playwright-stage manager, with a small San Francisco theatre, the Egyptian Hall, which specialized in trick work and presented a series of entertainments particularly calculated to satisfy its audience's appetite for the picturesque and exicting, the mysterious and bizarre. The "Egyptian Mystery," as the entertainment was called, featured among other things a variant of the famous "Pepper's Ghost" illusion, based on the principle of reflection. Belasco's own description of this technique is vivid: "There was a stage, covered with black velvet, and a sheet of glass, placed obliquely over a space beneath the stage— which was called the 'oven.' Gas lamps were ingeniously concealed so as to give the impression of a phosphorescent light from ghostlike bodies. The characters in the play were obliged to enter the 'oven' under the black velvet, and to lie on their backs, while their misty shadows were thrown like watery impressions upon the glass plate. As these shadows floated across the surface of the glass, the people in the 'oven' could easily shake tables and move chairs to the hair-raising satisfaction of the audience."[31]

Among other intriguing effects presented in the Egyptian Hall was a Faust and Valentine duel scene in which a sword "seemed to go *right through* the body of Faust."[32] The wonders of this theatre can, perhaps, best be appreciated by scanning one of its posters describing the varied marvels of a night's entertainment (Fig. 1). Hence the evening of April 10, 1877, began with a "New and Original Drama in 2 Acts (by a gentleman of this city)"—none other than Belasco—entitled *The Prodigal's Return, or The Father's Dream*. This piece was followed by a recitation accompanied by "a series of Wonderful Illusory Tableaux, illustrating the Life, Trials, Sickness and Death of *Little Jim! The Collier's Lad.*" The gripping scenic tableaux presented included: "(1) The Sick Child. (2)

The Mother's Prayer. (3) The Angel's Whisper. (4) The Collier's Return. (5) The Mother's Grief, and Tomb of Little Jim." These touching moments were further enhanced by special lighting effects designed "so that spirits seemed to float here and there, illustrating the sentiments of the lines."[33] The sorrowful interlude of Little Jim was succeeded by an appropriately moral playlet, *Storm of Thoughts*, "introducing another series of Illusions, which appear and disappear like phantoms from another world," and featuring such figures as Avica, Spirit of Avarice, Bac, Spirit of Wine, and the Fairy of Temperance. The drama spelled out the stoic and edifying "MORAL": "Man should be contented with his lot in life, and never seek to change." The evening was mercifully relieved by "the Laughable Farce of *Our Mysterious Boarding House*," which occasioned yet another display of "some Wonderful as well as Comical Illusions . . . representing the Mysterious and Diabolical proceedings of the Earthly and Unearthly."

Needless to say, the fame Belasco ultimately acquired as master of stage illusion rested on achievements of a quite different nature and artistic quality. Nonetheless, when twenty-five years later he staged the symbolic reunion of the dead lovers in *The Darling of the Gods* (1902), he created the unearthly, ethereal quality of this scene through the use of theatrical lighting to project a shadowy, floating stage picture reminiscent of the trick work in "Pepper's Ghost" and "Little Jim." In terms of sophistication, of course, the much admired scene in *The Darling of the Gods* cannot be compared with the lighting "illusions" of the "Egyptian Mysteries." If these early experiments are worth more than their value as comic relief, it is because

25

they were devised by a man with a unique sense of the future of lighting in the playhouse, a man who considered it his "fortune to come into the theatre during a time when lighting appliances and the use of illuminating effects were undergoing a great scientific revolution."[34]

The spectacular nature of other productions with which David Belasco was associated in San Francisco usually depended upon the use of extravaganza, lavish stage display, and special visual effects. This was the case with his adaptation of Watt Philips' *Not Guilty*, produced at the Baldwin in 1878 and billed in incandescent terms as "the Grand Production of the Magnificent, Musical, Military, Dramatic and Spectacular Christmas Piece."[35] Belasco's later recollection of the production in "My Life's Story" did nothing to minimize its colorful and lavish quality. "I introduced a battle scene," he recalled proudly, "with several hundred people in an embarkation, as well as horses and cannon. This embarkation alone used to take ten minutes. It has all been done in many plays since—the booming of guns, the padding of the horses' hoofs on earth and stone, the moving crowds in sight and larger ones suggested, beyond the range of vision—but this was the original, and it was wonderfully effective, if I do say it myself."[36]

The legendary but short-lived production at the San Francisco Grand Opera House of Salmi Morse's *The Passion Play* in 1879 once again gave Belasco free rein to revel in similar lavish effects and crowd arrangements on the grand scale. The production starred James O'Neill, type cast as Christ, a part, in the wicked words of William Winter, "to which he considered himself peculiarly fitted."[37] The spectacle offended many and ignited a verita-

26

ble public frenzy, culminating in the arrest of O'Neill on stage and a court injunction forbidding further performances of the play.[38] The reviewer for the *Argonaut* (March 8, 1879) began by describing the performance as "a series of beautiful tableaux and inspiring music." "The costumes, the chorus, the tableaux, the music were arranged with a taste that is beyond cavil," this critic declared, but concluded by damning the religious representation as "blasphemous, desecrating, unholy." Undaunted, meanwhile, Belasco used the occasion to explore every accessible possibility for pictorial display, searching for paintings that could be copied and for suggestions about costume, color and realistic atmosphere. "I went to the Mercantile Library and there studied the color effects in the two memorable canvases there hung, depicting the dance of Salomé and the Lord's Supper," he recalled. "In the Massacre of the Innocents we had a hundred mothers on the stage, with their babes in their arms. In the scene where Joseph and Mary came down the mountain side we had a flock of real sheep following in their wake."[39] The whole production is a typical illustration of the nineteenth-century emphasis on picturesque groupings and folk scenes, highlighted by colorful costumes and atmospheric surroundings. Its vivid panoramas were made further remarkable through the lighting effects introduced by Belasco for the first time. He eliminated the floats, or footlights, and lit his stage from the front with old locomotive bull's-eye lanterns, strung along the balcony railing, to obtain the effect of level rays. In carrying out this unusual experiment, he actually anticipated the methods of Reinhardt and Granville Barker by more than a quarter of a century.

In addition to scenery, props, and lighting, musical accompaniment was, as already suggested, a crucial element in the evocation of atmosphere in the theatre of Belasco's early days. It was used to enhance the festive or solemn mood of a Shakespearean performance. It stimulated the appropriate excitement in the production of melodramas and other plays. And it obviously played a predominant part in the production of the popular vaudevilles. Belasco's wide exposure during his San Francisco period to this aspect of theatrical production made him keenly aware of its advantages in effectively establishing scenic mood. In the 1882 production at the Baldwin of his own altered adaptation of Boucicault's celebrated antislavery drama *The Octoroon*, Belasco introduced the songs of the famous "Calender's Colored Minstrels" into the play. These entertainers lent an air of authenticity to the scenes in the cotton field and around the slave quarters. "Extraordinarily picturesque and impressive" was a scene in the last act which depicted the slaves slowly making their way home at night, singing as they moved through the cotton fields.[40] The use of music remained an important constituent of David Belasco's mature theatrical style, utilized not as a superimposed atmospheric accompaniment to the action, as in *The Octoroon*, but as a plastic value, closely integrated into the texture of the production as a whole. Musicality and rhythmic sense were key factors in Belasco's scenic art.

Perhaps the factor most clearly foreshadowing Belasco's later production style is his early manipulation of realistic detail to achieve the closest possible approximation to actual reality. His 1879 production of his own adaptation of Zola's *L'Assomoir* provides an illuminating comparison between the two men who were moving toward the creation of a new standard in the American theatre. Augustin Daly, who saw the original Paris performance of the French dramatization of Zola's novel at the Théâtre Ambigu-Comique in January of the same year and produced it in New York in April, described his impression of it in unsympathetic terms: "*L'Assomoir* is a disgusting piece—one prolonged sigh from first to last, over the miseries of the poor, with a dialogue culled from the lowest slang and tritest claptrap. . . . The only novelty in it was the *lavoir* scene, where two washwomen (the heroine and her rival) throw pails of warm water (actually) over each other and stand dripping before the audience."[41] Belasco, meanwhile, approached the play with enthusiasm. The San Francisco production, like the world première in Paris, reached a culmination of external reality in the washhouse scene. The actresses, Lillian Andrews and Rose Coghlan, were in a literal paroxysm of rage at the dress rehearsal. Both, relates Belasco, were "underdressed with close-fitting rubber suits to keep dry; but, even so, it was no fun to be drenched with hot soapy water, and I was sorry for them. But, of course, the scene had to be properly and fully rehearsed . . . everything was marvellously realistic."[42] While Daly's New York presentation was a complete failure, Belasco's direction made the San Francisco production a success. A single comparative incident, related by William Winter, is significant and suggestive. In Daly's version the fall of the male lead, Copeau, from a ladder was obviously accomplished by substituting a dummy figure for the actor who played the part. In Belasco's production this fall was so skillfully managed that "on opening night it was for several moments supposed by the audience that an actual accident had occurred."[43]

In a similar manner other plays which Belasco adapted and directed achieved their best effects through details that captured and astonished their audiences by their realistic credibility. In the mystery drama *Within an Inch of His Life* (1879), written in collaboration with James A. Herne and starring James O'Neill, Belasco created a sensation with a "terrific fire spectacle" that fully resembled real flames (but which utilized lighting rather than conventional chemical processes). "The fire was in the first act," he relates. "I did away with the lycopodium boxes and made my 'flames' by a series of red and yellow strips of silk, fanned from beneath by bellows and lit by colored lights. Some complaint was made of danger to the theatre, and the authorities came upon the stage to investigate; they were a good deal surprised at finding the 'fire' nothing but pieces of silk."[44] In the production of *Chums*, a sentimental version of the Enoch Arden story written in collaboration with James A. Herne and later renamed *Hearts of Oak*, Belasco evoked both the admiration and astonishment of his audience by employing real water, real beans, real boiled potatoes, and various other components of a real supper, as well as a real cat and a real, and apparently rather discontented, baby on the stage.[45]

Belasco's early career abounds with examples of stage effects similar to these. They became part of the legend that quickly grew up around his theatre and his colorful, theatrical personality. "The great Wizard," as Alexander Woollcott enjoyed calling him in his reviews, belonged wholly to the world of the theatre. He had a total understanding of how to create effect, not only in a production but also around his own person, which bore a stamp of exoticism and mysticism he assiduously strove to preserve.

Throughout the greater part of his career Belasco continued to wear the stand-up collar of his youth on the West Coast. This, accented by a black ascot and dark, severe suits, lent his appearance an eccentrically ecclesiastical authority further enhanced by a dark, foreign, almost oriental appearance. Persistent reports, willingly endorsed by their subject, had it that he had adopted his dress out of veneration for a Catholic priest, a shadowy Father McGuire, who had tutored the Jewish boy during his eventful childhood. Similar stories about the world behind Belasco's scenes and the charismatic, Svengali-like personality of Mr. B himself were legion, and are still told by those who remember him. From time to time the public was permitted glimpses, through newspaper articles and pictures, of the opulent theatricalism pervading the backstage "Studio," the inner sanctum from which the Belasco necromancy emanated. The incredible lengths to which he would go, the tireless labor he would expend to perfect a production became proverbial. Other rumors, sometimes denied by Belasco, sometimes not, whispered that his notably effective training of famous performers—particularly actresses—veritably took place by the stroke of the lash. The strange, exciting, imposing persona behind these tales soon surrounded himself with a luminous theatrical aura that made the ordinary realities of the world seem drab indeed.[46]

THE YEAR 1882 marked a decisive turning point in David Belasco's career. His play, *La Belle Russe*, described by the *New York Times* (May 9, 1882) as "the story of an exceedingly audacious woman, known at one time among the gamblers and *roués* of Europe as 'la Belle Russe.' " was accepted by New York's foremost producer, Lester Wallack, and performed at his theatre. The *Tribune* (May 9, 1882) called it "a most interesting exposition of monstrous feminine wickedness. . . . It suggests to the moralist the curious spectacle of hellish depravity stumbling among its own self-justification." The *Times,* on the other hand, found the play "one of those unreal, unreasonable things which are not meant to impose upon a sane intelligence; but it has elements of theatrical interest which have lifted many plays, even more unnatural plays than *La Belle Russe,* into popular favor." The latter prediction proved correct, and Belasco's drama became an immediate popular success. It was revived by Wallack in the following season, was sent on tour in 1885 under the management of Charles Frohman, and was produced in London the following year. More important, however, Wallack's successful production of the play, combined with the intervention of the Frohman brothers, helped to establish its author within the year as resident director of one of America's leading theatres, the Madison Square Theatre in New York.

As his faithful biographer William Winter emphasizes, meanwhile, before Belasco embarked upon his New York career "he had seen much of the best acting of his period and had been intimately associated with many leaders of the stage—sometimes as a student and assistant, sometimes as adviser and director. He had acted, in all sorts of circumstances and in all sorts of places, more than 170 parts. He had altered, adapted, rewritten, or written more than 100 plays and he had been the responsible director in the production of more than three times that number."[47]

The foregoing kaleidoscope of genres and influences to which Belasco was exposed during his early years in California suggests, then, a context indispensable in evaluating the maturation of the aims and methods of his scenic art. The later work of Belasco as a dramatist and director had its roots in the immense practical experience and the wide exposure to styles and trends which this context provided. These early experiences and impressions were, however, supplemented or supplanted by a host of others as Belasco's career entered a new and more important phase.

## CHAPTER TWO

# *Transition*

THE YEARS IN SAN FRANCISCO served primarily as a period of education for David Belasco, as a prologue to the artistically and stylistically more significant productions he subsequently mounted. During the earlier period he had shown a flair for realistic illusion and had displayed a creative ingenuity which had set him apart. It was not until he came to New York in 1882, however, that his reputation in the theatre became firmly established and his distinct style as a naturalist developed in earnest. Belasco became America's foremost exponent of a theatrical style in which all the individual elements of a production, from text to setting, props, lighting, and acting, operate as completely integrated parts subordinate to the larger, realistic whole. Belasco represented a unique quality in the theatre because he combined a thorough, practical knowledge of acting with experience as a director, a producer, and a playwright. His mind grasped all phases of a production and visualized it as a totality. He was able, as few have been, to realize to the utmost degree the ideal of a theatre dominated by a single intelligence controlling text, scenery, and lights, training and directing the actors, and thereby achieving a complete and unique artistic unity.

During nearly half a century of association with the New York theatre, Belasco was connected with 123 Broadway productions. From 1882 Belasco functioned as playwright and stage manager-director for the Mallory Brothers, owners of the Madison Square Theatre. He left this theatre in 1885, supporting himself for two years as a free-lance dramatist, director, and acting teacher. Significantly, his departure from the Madison Square Theatre was prompted by a dispute over his self-determined right to be the sole authority presiding at rehearsals.[1] In 1887 Belasco joined the Lyceum, again as a playwright, a director, and a teacher in the theatre's acting school (later the American Academy of Dramatic Arts). Not yet his own master, however, and determined to become an independent force in the theatre, he left the Lyceum in 1890. During the following five years he established a considerable reputation, both as a dramatist and a director, on a free-lance basis. In 1895 the production of his Civil War drama, *The Heart of Maryland*, which starred his pupil, Mrs. Leslie Carter, marked his emergence as an independent producer. From that date until the end of his career, Belasco worked entirely on his own, presenting only plays that interested him and evolving a uniquely personal production style. In 1902 he acquired his own theatre by taking over the Republic which, after a complete remodeling and modernization, was renamed the Belasco. In 1907 he acquired a second Broadway house, the magnificently appointed Stuyvesant, which was built under his personal direction. (In October, 1910, Belasco gave his name to the Stuyvesant, and the Republic reverted to its original name.)

The gradual evolution of David Belasco's naturalistic production principles was closely linked to certain significant practical factors. It was shaped not only by fashions and conventions encountered in the California theatre of his early years, but also by newer developments which marked the period of his transition to the New York theatre. Chief among these transitional developments were the physical characteristics of the new theatres in which he worked—particularly the revolutionary introduction of electric lighting—and the new type of drama to which he was exposed.

The development of the naturalistic style in the European theatre became, in many cases, intimately connected with the establishment of small stages. Strindberg's celebrated preface to *Miss Julie* (1888) called specifically for a small theatre, like that later exemplified by the *Intima Teatern* in Stockholm, founded in 1907 and seating 161 spectators (although Strindberg actually wanted a theatre with 400 to 500 seats), or by Antoine's *Théâtre Libre* on Montmartre, which seated 343 spectators. "If we, first and foremost, could have an intimate stage and an intimate theatre," asserted Strindberg, complaining of the unrealistic and unsubtle effects produced in theatres of large dimensions, "then we may see the inception of a new drama, and the theatre could again become an institution for the entertainment of the cultured." The small theatre in which audience and actors were in close rapport constituted an important prerequisite for the naturalistic style of performance. It provided the opportunity for a development

36

towards a more subdued diction, less pronounced stage gestures and plastique, and a more realistic pattern of stage movement. In short, it helped to facilitate a kind of playing which drew its life from an intimate milieu, realistically depicted on the stage on at least a somewhat authentic scale.

It is therefore a critical clue in understanding Belasco's makeup as a naturalistic director that the two theatres with which he was chiefly connected during his eight formative years in New York, the Madison Square Theatre and the Lyceum, were both very small. The Madison Square is today remembered principally for Steele Mac-Kaye's double elevator stage, installed in 1880 to facilitate very rapid changes of scene—a solution to the problem posed by the increasing use of the box set to reproduce interior scenes in detail.[2] This theatre was also remarkable, however, for its intimate dimensions, accommodating only 700 spectators. By comparison, the magnificent Booth's Theatre built eleven years earlier had a seating capacity of no less than 1,750, and provided standing room for an additional 300 spectators.[3] The Lyceum Theatre, also built by MacKaye and opened in 1885, was in many respects revolutionary. Its overall dimensions were small, with a seating capacity of only 614, and it was lighted by electricity.[4]

Similarly, when David Belasco acquired his own theatres they were also both relatively intimate in their dimensions. "I like a moderate sized, even a small theatre, for most plays," Belasco stated explicitly, "because of the intimacy, the close contact which permits the closest observation, so that the most delicate and subtle touches, intonations and glances, the fluttering of an eyelid, the trembling of a lip, the tense tremor of nervous fingers, shall not be lost or obscured."[5] The first Belasco Theatre seated 950 spectators, including 450 on the main orchestra floor, 200 in the balcony, and 300 in the gallery; the second Belasco (Stuyvesant) accommodated an audience of just over one thousand, assigning 450 to the orchestra floor, 320 to the balcony, and 240 to the gallery. The richly dark yet subdued color scheme of both auditoriums further reinforced their intimate atmosphere. The interior of the first Belasco Theatre was decorated in muted shades of red, green, deep brown, and gold, while in the still more opulent Belasco-Stuyvesant the color accents blended dark browns, blues, and greens with dull amber and orange.[6]

As photographs from Belasco's productions in both of his theatres indicate, stage dimensions in them were also relatively modest. In the Belasco-Stuyvesant the proscenium opening was thirty-two feet wide and thirty feet high; the distance from the curtain line to the back wall measured twenty-seven feet. In 1915 this stage was enlarged by the addition of a five-foot apron in front of the curtain line. Both of Belasco's theatres were equipped with elaborate mechanical aids to facilitate the setting and shifting of scenery. Each had a large fly gallery complete with counterweight machinery designed to ease the shifting of Belasco's heavy, three-dimensional scenery. In each, moreover, the entire acting area was serviced by a number of small traps surrounding a sizeable central elevator trap (measuring thirty feet in length by fifteen feet in depth in the first Belasco Theatre, and twenty feet by ten in the Belasco-Stuyvesant), upon which the entire trappings of a scene could be lowered to, or raised from, the

38

basement underneath the stage. Once in the basement, this central platform, constructed like a large, moveable wagon, could be rolled aside and replaced by another similar section which was then raised to stage level, loaded with the elements needed for the following scene. With the help of this flexible system, which combined vertical and horizontal movement, the shifting of even the heaviest and most elaborately built up and furnished sets could be accomplished in minimum time in Belasco's technically sophisticated playhouses.[7] In addition, the lighting methods and equipment employed on both of his stages were of an impressively complex and revolutionary nature.

The incentive to subtler acting methods furnished by smaller stages was given an added and decisive impetus with the introduction of electric stage lighting. For Belasco the appearance of the incandescent lamp in 1879 opened up a whole new field of opportunity. "It is usual to consider the inventions of Thomas A. Edison from the viewpoint of their scientific, commercial, and practical utility. We of the theatre," Belasco pointed out, "realize how great also is the debt which the dramatic producer's art owes for its present perfection to this magician. It was inevitable that I should utilize to the fullest extent every means by which the true effects of nature could be more closely reproduced in the theatre. So it is upon applying to the stage's art electric lighting, and the more perfect use of color which it has made possible, that a great part of my thought and energies as a dramatic producer has been concentrated."[8]

In addition to influencing performance style, electric lighting created changes in the entire scenic picture. It thereby became possible to introduce natural effects with a subtlety and variation in light, shadow, and coloring previously inconceivable on the stage. Furthermore, it placed new demands upon the illusionistic quality of the setting. What could pass for reality on the dimly lit, pre-electric stage was now brutally unmasked in the brighter, more intense electric lighting. As lighting improved, moreover, the possibility of visually integrating the figure of the actor with the obviously two-dimensional, painted scenery quickly decreased. The reaction to the inadequacy of painted sets resulted in a movement towards a greater use of plastic, three-dimensional detail. "There is nothing so hard to find on stage as an interior set that comes close to looking as a room *should* look," asserted Strindberg in his famous plea for realistic stage settings. "We may have to tolerate walls made of canvas, but it is about time that we stopped having shelves and kitchen utensils painted on it. There are so many other conventions on stage that strain our imagination; certainly we might be freed from overexerting ourselves in an effort to believe that pots and pans painted on the scenery are real." While Strindberg attempted to make the action of plays like *Miss Julie* realistically acceptable *despite* stage settings made of canvas that moved at the slightest touch, Belasco took the full consequence of the new craving for realism, requiring, as we shall see, that everything on his stage should be absolutely authentic and true-to-life. No longer was the setting to be merely "appropriate," a favorite adjective of the producer in the romantic period, nor was it to function simply as a splendid or picturesque background. It now had to be both truly and significantly "real," as obviously solid and substantial as though plucked from life itself.

This desire to create the illusion of a slice of reality behind the proscenium arch, a reality which the audience would recognize and accept in its minutest detail, presupposed a meticulous artistic discipline which would not have been possible for Belasco to achieve during his earlier San Francisco period. The stock-company system of production dominant there generally required that a new play should be presented every two weeks. "It was taken for granted," Belasco recalled later, "that I should get a play ready for rehearsal in less than a week, and put it on in less than another week."[9] Under such conditions, any given production could receive only very limited care and attention. Also in this respect, however, a transition was taking place, and when Belasco arrived in New York, conditions there had changed. "By good fortune my work in the New York theatre, with its wider facilities, began about the time of the transition from the stock-company system of presenting plays to productions which were made with a view to greater permanence, in which more careful attention could be given to the details of their staging," he pointed out.[10]

A significant factor in this transition from the stock-company system was the introduction of the so-called "combination" system. In the 1860s America had acquired a network of railways which made possible the touring of a single, complete production with its full cast. At first, few companies were involved in these road shows. As Belasco indicates, however, the eighties marked a period of change. Before this time every major city had its resident stock company, capable of mounting a large repertory each season with its own actors, as well as supporting the touring stars. Although the "combination" system still took advantage of the drawing power of the star, he was now supported by his own traveling company. The emphasis shifted to the presentation of individual productions complete in themselves. Ultimately, the new system brought about a weakening of the old stock-company approach which has been much lamented by critics and historians of the American theatre. Nevertheless, the emergence at this time of new production standards, especially the concepts of specifically detailed stage environments and carefully rehearsed ensemble playing, had already begun to undermine the versatile repertory system of the stock companies and render it artistically obsolete.

Belasco's demand for theatrical totality and his attention to detail characterized not only his own New York productions, but eventually influenced the standard of artistic accomplishment in the American theatre as a whole. He "brought to that theatre a standard of tidiness in production and maturation of manuscript, a standard that has discouraged to no little extent that theatre's erstwhile not uncommon frowsy hustle and slipshod manner of presentation," his otherwise harshest critic, George Jean Nathan, was compelled to admit.[11] It was due in no small way to Belasco's efforts to create integrated artistic unity in theatrical production, and to combat all aspects of poor or half-hearted scenic workmanship, that the noteworthy guest performances from abroad which appeared in New York between 1911 and 1922 did not seem like light coming to a dark land. Audiences were prepared to judge the art of Dublin's Abbey Players, Copeau's Vieux Colombier, Granville Barker, Max Reinhardt, and the Moscow Art Theatre on a level with that already presented on the New York stage. Thus, Stark Young remarked that the production techniques of the Moscow Art Theatre, which appeared in New York in 1923, represented "what we have had on hand for a generation or more."[12]

Finally, in addition to technical resources and developments, the creation of verisimilitude on the stage was obviously directly conditioned by the type of repertoire being performed. The plays on which Belasco worked, as a director or a playwright or both, during his early years in New York were for the most part dramas in modern dress, presenting what at that time was regarded as a convincing picture of contemporary conditions and contemporary society. The first play he directed at the Madison Square Theatre was Bronson Howard's *Young Mrs. Winthrop*, a drama which, in the opinion of Arthur Hobson Quinn, "placed on the stage for the first time in America a group of characters, whose actions are determined by the power of social laws and the interruptions of social distractions, without making the prevailing note one of satire."[13] In 1884 Belasco followed this pattern with his own *May Blossom*, a well-made, sentimental society play which achieved an ultimate distinction of sorts: a cigar was named for it with the characteristic slogan, "a play without a broken heart would hardly draw—a cigar that will not draw is an abomination!"[14] During the Lyceum period, the plays that Belasco directed and wrote in collaboration with Henry C. De Mille are particularly noteworthy. *The Wife* (1887), *Lord Chumley* (1888), *The Charity Ball* (1889), and *Men and Women* (1890) were hailed by the critics for their treatment of contemporary New York subject matter and their natural stage dialogue, and the environment they depicted on stage was made pictorially and dramatically effective by Belasco's judicious use of integrated realistic detail to evoke a valid scenic milieu.[15]

"Our productions at the Lyceum were marked by great simplicity of treatment. There was no attempt to be theatrical. We used to depict life as the men and women who came to see it experienced it. There was no cut and dried staginess," Belasco later proudly recalled. "We on the Fourth Avenue gave allegiance to the so-called 'society' drama. In this line we surpassed all other theatres in this city."[16]

In the spectacular San Francisco productions with which Belasco had been associated, his more or less close attention to detail was aimed primarily at increasing the purely picturesque effect of a performance by lending it a splash of authentically local, historical, or exotic color. This kind of effort added a dimension of wonder to the proceedings on stage, a dimension which, of course, relates to the general cult of the wondrous and the strange which permeated the older romantic theatre. Such an element was certainly not absent from the nineteenth-century contemporary dress productions that Belasco staged in New York. The melodramas he directed and adapted had as their inherent purpose the creation of a heightened effect of surprise and suspense, both in the staging and in the dramatic action. In the newer type of repertoire, however, the use of realistic detail not only established the desired atmosphere and background; it also gave the stage action a contemporaneous and immediate realistic credibility. Hence these plays in contemporary guise, depicting characters behaving as in "real" life, surrounded by real objects, contributed most directly to paving the way for a naturalistic production style in which individualized, concrete details were integrated into a convincingly true-to-life, recognizable milieu.

It is significant that Belasco's transition from California to New York was dominated from the outset by such a contemporary repertory. Following this period of transition, he produced plays which ranged in style from historical or oriental-exotic authenticity to American frontier drama and social realism. One basic artistic aim in mounting these varied types of productions was, however, predominant: the achievement of naturalistic verisimilitude. For Belasco, meticulous outer realism remained throughout his career the key to the inner reality of a play. His artistic intentions and contributions as a naturalist, the vision and method of his scenic art, can, meanwhile, be examined most profitably not in chronological terms but by means of a cross-analysis of the principal aspects of his mature production style.

## CHAPTER THREE

# *Vision and Method*

"BEYOND THE MARGIN of a miniature the whole world can be seen, if the miniature is faithful."[1] These words of Belasco epitomize, not without eloquence, his belief in the efficacy of presenting an utterly "faithful" miniature of life on his stage. Belasco's talent lay first and foremost in his eminent ability to exercise theatrical persuasion. The plays he produced were chosen or written by him with a sharp sense of the practical theatre and a concrete image of that theatre invariably in mind. His repertoire consisted not of literary masterpieces but chiefly of romantic, sentimental "well-made plays" and melodramas. Belasco himself was keenly aware of their primarily theatrical value. It was his deep conviction that the terms "literature" and "theatre" had very little in common with each other. "The literary drama is very beautiful—for the library shelves," he wrote with characteristic irony. "It lives, of course—on the library shelves. But it is not actable, because it does not get beneath the vest. So I am not literary, because my target is the emotions."[2] Or, elsewhere: "The

46

province of literature is entirely outside the province of the theatre."[3]

Hence David Belasco had little regard for what he termed "the heavy German style of intellectual drama," in which category he classed Hauptmann and Ibsen. The critic James Gibbons Huneker, writing at the end of his life, remembered quizzing Belasco about "the Moderns" (Ibsen, Hauptmann, Maeterlinck, Becque) and found that he "knew all these revolutionists; he still reads them, as his library shelves show. He knows more about the practical side of Ibsen (for he admires the great Norwegian's supreme mastery of dramatic technique) than do his own faultfinders among the so-called amateur pocket playhouses." Though he admired Ibsen's technical skill, however, Belasco was ill at ease with his somberness. He belonged instead, in Huneker's view, to "the great dramatic traditions of the golden age. Shakespeare is his god. Then the romantic French theatre. And little wonder. Sentiments more than ideas are the pabulum of his plays."[4]

The American theatre-goer, Belasco believed, had no wish to see deep spiritual searching portrayed on the stage, but rather "action—plenty of action," a variety of passions, attitudes, and emotions.[5] This view does, moreover, suggest an interesting comparison with the principles of George Pierce Baker's *Dramatic Technique* (1919), a book based squarely on the assumption that " 'from emotions to emotions' is the formula for any good play. . . . The emotions to be reached are those of the audience. The emotions conveyed are those of the people on the stage."[6] It was Belasco's basic and frequently reiterated conviction that "American audiences have always and always will

47

demand plays that depict life—not ideal life perhaps, but life as they know it."[7] In 1893 the *New York Times* (January 26) succinctly characterized the public of this gilded age of American industrial expansion and profit accumulation as one "which cares very little for either poetry or satire, which is never pessimistic, and is restless under the influence of literary hair-splitting, but which, in this big town, is not so very easily pleased for all that." Belasco instinctly understood this, and his productions did succeed in pleasing this public, which is to say that they were true to life as their contemporary audiences desired or believed it to be.[8]

The repertory which Belasco presented as a New York director falls into at least three distinct categories. Following his early collaboration with De Mille on the plays depicting a typical New York society milieu, his taste swung toward plays more closely related to the environment and the repertory he had known during his years on the West Coast. Thus vivid, colorful panoramas of Western life in America—*The Girl I Left behind Me* (with Franklyn Fyles, 1893), *The Heart of Maryland* (1895), *The Rose of the Rancho* (with R. W. Tully, 1906), and chiefly, *The Girl of the Golden West* (1905)—constitute one important category in his repertory and his scenic style.[9]

This type of play was supplemented by a second group of exotic or historical romances and extravaganzas, starting with *Madame Butterfly* (1900) and followed by *Du Barry* (1901), *The Darling of the Gods* (with John Luther Long, 1902), *Sweet Kitty Bellairs* (1903), and *Adrea* (with Long, 1905).

Meanwhile, Belasco also continued the line of domestic

milieu dramas with such productions as Lee Arthur and Charles Klein's *The Auctioneer* (1901), Klein's *The Music Master* (1904), and his own *The Return of Peter Grimm* (1911). Within this category of contemporary domestic dramas, those oriented toward an outspoken social realism, chiefly *Zaza* (1899), adapted by Belasco from a French play by Pierre Berton and Charles Simon, and Eugene Walter's *The Easiest Way* (1909), hold particular interest.

These earlier plays, which constituted the broad base of Belasco's repertoire, were nearly all revived by him several times in the course of his career. The plays which he produced after 1915—with the possible exception of Brieux's *L'Avocat*, performed as *The Accused* (1925), *Deburau* (1920), Granville Barker's adaptation of Sacha Guitry, and *Mima* (1928), Belasco's own adaptation of Ferenc Molnar's *The Red Mill*—are of generally less stylistic significance. Although most of them were great popular successes and Belasco went on directing until barely six months before his death in May 1931, none of these later productions contributes new or important characteristics to his physiognomy as a director and producer. However, a unique phase of Belasco's work is represented by his 1922 production of *The Merchant of Venice*, his sole venture into the area of Shakespearean production, regarded by many as the crowning achievement of his artistic career. In the chapters which follow, productions representative of each of the main categories just described will be analyzed in some detail.

As a theorist Belasco was, as his selection of a dramatic repertoire suggests, deeply anchored in the most solidly entrenched ideas of the nineteenth century. As a practical theatre man, however, he was distinctly a spirit of prog-

ress. An analysis of phases of his scenic technique, his technical discoveries, and not least his experiments with stage
lighting points clearly forward towards a period which is
considered revolutionary in American theatre, the period
of the emergence of the New Stagecraft in the 1920s. It is
in this context that his artistic contributions must be
viewed.

FOR DAVID BELASCO the principle that "the drama's laws the
drama's patrons give" remained incontestable. His plays
were shaped with an audience in mind, in the spirit of
George Jean Nathan's classic remark: "Good drama is
anything that interests an intelligently emotional group
of persons assembled together in an illuminated hall."[10]
Belasco had a deep and instinctive sense for what would
interest an audience. "I believe that no other producer had
such a gift of anticipating the reaction of the audience of
any given transaction on the stage," asserted his associate,
Daniel Frohman.[11]

Much in the spirit of the French writers of well-made
plays, Belasco himself insisted upon being called a "playwright" rather than a "dramatist." A reporter, who in
1894 asked him for a reason for this fact, received the reply: "Simply because it is the proper term. A wright is a
workman. We say wheelwright, shipwright . . . why not
playwright? A wright takes the materials he finds to his
hand and builds or forms them into a coherent shape. He
makes nothing; he only puts them together more or less
deftly. The materials he works with are scattered around.
He takes them, chips them, varnishes them, fits them into
place, and so erects his structure."[12]

Belasco felt no compulsion to place problems under debate on the stage. "I believe in the play that deals with life in its moments of importance, in a crisis of emotion," was his credo.[13] As a rule his plays centered about feelings, moods, or situations, and not about moral, social, or ethical questions. Hence it was possible for champions of an artistic and social realism unencumbered by the artificial conflicts of the "well-made play" to raise numerous objections to the dramas he presented. Belasco's action-packed Civil War play *The Heart of Maryland*, which established him as an independent producer in 1895 and which was performed in London in 1898 with Mrs. Leslie Carter in the title role, was hardly destined to delight the progressive critical spirit of a George Bernard Shaw. Shaw's reaction to the production is an early foreshadowing of the view of Belasco's dramaturgy that subsequently evolved in America.

Bernard Shaw was by no means blind to the theatrical merits of *The Heart of Maryland*. "The actors know the gymnastics of their business," he wrote, "and work harder and more smartly, and stick to it better than English actors. Mrs. Leslie Carter is a melodramatic heroine of no mean power . . . her transports and tornadoes, in which she shews plenty of professional temperament and susceptibility, give intensity to the curtain situations and secure her a flattering series of recalls." It was the play's content which he castigated. He found the sweeping heroism of its somewhat romanticized view of the war between North and South "despicable, puerile and blackguardly"; its undifferentiated portrayal of ugly villainy was branded by him as "mechanical criminality." With customary nonchalance he ascribed the drama's force to "a combination of descriptive talent with delirium tremens." The realism of its action placed him in "a cold sweat of pity and terror." "Imagine going to war," Shaw declared, "with a stock of patriotic idealism and national enthusiasm instead of a stock of military efficiency."[14] When the American critic George Jean Nathan mounted his attack on Belasco, he employed a similarly corrosive and witty approach in his customary, conscious effort to copy Shaw.

Belasco, however, had no interest in this kind of cold, analytical discussion of content—particularly not by Shaw, whom he dismissed as "a quick-witted Irishman without respect for the most sacred things of life and, withal, a poser."[15] Belasco's view of what lends meaning and value to a theatrical event was determined solely by his attitude toward practical theatre. In the preface to the first edition of a collection of his own plays, he presented his view of drama very succinctly: "In permitting the publication of these plays of mine in this form, I am aware of sacrificing the glamour of the stage; I realize that I 'show the puppets dallying,' that I 'pluck out the heart of the mystery'. . . . The standards by which true literature is judged cannot be properly applied in judging drama. . . . My plays are all written to be acted, not to be read."[16]

Belasco's initial concern was with new theatrical form rather than with new dramatic content. A play text was to him primarily a starting point for directorial elaboration. Returning to *The Heart of Maryland*, the effect was, in the words of the *New York Times* (October 27, 1895), "largely, vividly, splendidly pictorial." This quality, achieved by means of minute attention to realistic detail, movement, sound, and light, gave vigor and distinction to the stage action and highlighted its emotional impact. The *Times* reviewer recaptured in lively terms his impression of the production: "We hear the tramp of infantry, the clatter of cavalry and the rumble of artillery. The boom and rattle of distant conflict are heard. The sun shines golden yellow and the moon pale. Their light falls on the veranda and dooryard of a mansion . . . on the Maryland hills, and on an old gray church battered by shells. The church is used as a prison, and whenever a prisoner escapes, the church bell is rung to warn the pickets, who then make short work of him."

The memorable scene which presented Mrs. Carter heroically climbing the bell tower, grasping the clapper of the great bell, and then swinging to and fro to prevent the sounding of an alarm that would mean the capture of her lover was recalled by Belasco's contemporaries, among them his colleague Charles Frohman, as "the most thrilling scene" he ever created in the theatre.[17] The height of excitement was reached as the indomitable heroine sped up the stairs to the belfry to save her lover, played by the dashing Maurice Barrymore, from capture as a Union spy. The stage directions from Belasco's promptbook for the play vividly describe the bold emotionality and picturesque suspense of the episode, containing only a few snatches of spoken dialogue but requiring a complete stage set. "The belfry. The bell is *C*. A ladder comes up from below. The light of the moon falls on the bell. . . . Maryland is seen as she climbs the ladder. She has a lighted lantern in her hand which she throws away when she reaches the second story of the belfry (from stage). With excited exclamation she rushes to the top story. As she is appearing through top opening, shouting from below. . . . *Ring the bell!* The ponderous tongue begins to move and strikes faintly the lip of the bell just as Maryland stands facing it. . . . Maryland leaps and clings with both hands to the tongue of the bell. The bell moves higher and higher; she is dragged backwards and forwards by the swing. Shouting etc. kept up until the curtain falls."[18]

Dramatically such a scene is obviously reminiscent of the venerable melodrama tradition of bodies roped to railway tracks, heroes in cellars where tidewater is rising, circular saws and steam hammers threatening the lives of helpless victims, and other overwhelming displays of high-minded virtue grappling with deep-dyed villainy.[19] *The Heart of Maryland* represents the taste for thrilling stage action which Belasco carried with him to New York from his early years in California. In the course of time, however, this taste underwent a marked change toward a more modified, subdued scheme of expression. Belasco's statement in 1911, "I am convinced that 'action' on the stage is wholly mental, and not at all physical," indicates the nature of the change which took place in his work.[20] It was reflected in his general choice of repertoire after 1895, in the reduction of animated outer action in his own plays and adaptations, and in his directorial theory and practice. For Belasco, meanwhile, such a change was prompted not by aesthetic considerations but primarily by practical ideas of theatrical performance.

Belasco epitomizes a period in American theatre in which theatrical effectiveness took precedence over all other considerations for a dramatist. He frequently expressed the view that from the very outset he had felt obliged to write parts in his plays which would reflect the talents of the actors engaged to appear in their presentation. From the beginning at the Lyceum, he told William Winter, "De Mille and I found ourselves obliged to create characters to fit the personalities of the players Mr. Frohman [Daniel Frohman, the manager] had engaged. We could not say: 'Here is our heroine. Find an actress to suit her'—for Georgia Cayvan was to be the leading lady, whatever the play might be, and it was for us to see that she had a womanly woman's part."[21] In the case of *Lord Chumley*, the play was not only conceived as a starring vehicle for Edward H. Sothern but also as an attempt to duplicate the elder Sothern's celebrated role as Lord Dundreary in *Our American Cousin*. As it turned out the idea was a very successful one. The efficacy of this method of playwriting and of Belasco's subsequent direction is illustrated by the fact that the Lyceum ensemble soon acquired a reputation as one of the finest in New York.[22] Similarly the plays which he afterwards wrote, adapted, or selected for production continued to be tailored to his company and the abilities of his performers, a fact recognized and accepted in numerous reviews of his performances.

Belasco's keen sense of theatrical values resulted in the fact that not merely situations and complications were usually planned in careful detail before a line of dramatic dialogue was written. Even the blocking itself, for instance the time it took for an actor to cross the stage, determined in a similar way the length and texture of a line to be spoken. Belasco constantly revised his plays during rehearsal if he found it necessary. "Almost invariably the exceptionally successful play is not written but rewritten," he explained. "However attractive it may seem in the form in which it comes to the producer, it is capable of improvement. This axiom of the theatre, which is as old as the theatre itself, has been verified again and again in my own experience."[23] As a director he demanded that other writers be equally willing to alter their plays according to his instructions. "Ways of improving it constantly suggest themselves," he emphasized. "If it seems too heavy at a certain point, it must be lightened; if too tearful, laughter must be brought into it. Not a dozen, but a hundred, little touches are sometimes possible."[24]

"Some characters in plays say lovely things about ten pages long," he declared elsewhere in an interview about his methods as a playwright. "In real life this would be absurd, and I try to portray real men and women."[25] Just as he objected to rhetoric and overly exalted feelings in the theatre, he also avoided dwelling too long on a single feeling or effect. Exaggerated, gross, or shocking effects repelled him. He found no purpose or value in the violent stimulation of an audience's emotions. This was, Huneker explains, the reason that a play like Strindberg's *Miss Julie* failed to appeal to him. "Why? Question of temperament. Its 'modernity' has nothing to do with the matter. It is, with all its shuddering power, too frank, too brutal for him. He demands the consoling veils of illusion to cover the nakedness of the human soul."[26] A sense of the harmonious and the conciliatory lay deeply rooted in Belasco, a sense that appears everywhere in his work and comes to expression in all phases of his theatrical activity.

Characteristic of these attitudes is the description of his creation of *The Return of Peter Grimm*, a play which represents both a high point in his writing career and an illustration of his special ability to plan dramatic action on the basis of theatrical values. The play, starring David Warfield in the title role, received its first New York performance at the second Belasco Theatre in 1911, where it continued to run for an impressive total of 231 consecutive performances. Reviewers were enthusiastic. "Mr. Belasco has never demonstrated more conclusively his genius than in this drama," declared the critic for the *Brooklyn Eagle* (October 18, 1911). "As a play *The Return of Peter Grimm* is entitled to rank as a remarkable dramatic achievement, but as an illustration of the art of Mr. Belasco in creating illusion, it ranks by far as the highest effort of his career." *Theatre Magazine* (November 1911) took delight in the play's "simplicity and truth in the impossible circumstances that are made actual."

The drama deals, in Belasco's own words, with "the persistent survival of personality, or, as some people would have it, a ghost."[27] The action and the main idea of the play necessitate the fact that the spirit of its title figure, a Dutch greenhouse owner, becomes visible to one of the characters. Peter Grimm returns to repair a mistake he has committed in life which has blighted the romance and threatens to destroy the happiness of his niece. A note in the program for the production stressed the fact that the play was not intended to advance any theory regarding the probability of the return of the main character. "For the many it may be said that he could exist only in the minds of the characters grouped about him—in their subconscious memories. For the few, his presence will embody the theory of the survival of persistent personal energy." Reflecting the realist's penchant for "research," the note added that "a conversation with Professor [William] James of Harvard, and the works of Professor Hyslop, of the American branch of the London Society of Psychical Research, have also aided Mr. Belasco."

Belasco's efforts in connection with *The Return of Peter*

*Grimm* were directed wholly toward the relation of the dramatic story in realistically plausible scenic terms. In presenting the return of Peter's spirit, he first introduced a seance scene with a female medium, but at rehearsals this method struck him as ridiculous. Experiments with numerous other possibilities followed, none of which succeeded in satisfying him, until he hit upon the idea of introducing a new character into the play: a small eight-year-old boy who, when he dies at the close of the play, sees the presence of Peter's spirit and brings his message to the others. Belasco sought to ameliorate the painful effect which the little boy's death scene might have on the audience by including an effective contrast in the opening scene. Here, a circus parade passes the house where the action takes place, a circus band playing and clowns singing, to the delight of the small boy standing at the window and watching the procession go by. One of the clowns suddenly leaps through the open window and dances about with little Willem. Peter Grimm sends the lad off with the clown to buy tickets to the circus (Fig. 2). In the death scene at the conclusion, the circus sounds were all repeated, "phantom circus music . . . with its elfin horns," softly and far away as if "faint images of Willem's dream." When Willem "dies," he simply climbs onto Peter's shoulders and rides off with him, singing "Uncle Rat," the circus melody he learned from the clown in the first act.[28]

By means of this suggestive effect Belasco succeeded in projecting his conception of the play in a manner that was moving without being painful or sensational. The events were carefully balanced against each other. A unified impression characterized by harmony and equilibrium as well as ultimate theatricality was achieved. This technique of balance stamps not only individual elements but also the structure of the play as a whole.

In the first act of *The Return of Peter Grimm* the audience is introduced to the title figure and is made to feel sympathy for him, partly because of his whimsical and kindly nature and partly because of the malicious and concealed opposition of his nephew. Peter learns that he has only a short time to live. But this tense situation is immediately contrasted with the gaiety of the passing circus parade mentioned above. Shadow and light are boldly juxtaposed, and the overall effect is made more intense than if no such contrast had occurred.

The final scene in the play is marked by a similar conciliatory atmosphere. Belasco escapes the bathos which might result from a realistic death scene, and the intended moods of bittersweetness, of mystery, and of realization of the import of Peter's message that death is "knowing better" are projected through the use of the visual and sound devices just described. The fact that Belasco suspends the conventional, photographic approach to such a scene and substitutes a technique of suggestive realism constitutes one of the many instances in his theatrical method which points ahead toward the future use of symbolic elements in a production.

## STAGING

WHEN IT CAME to the external presentation of a play, David Belasco was a naturalist to the fingertips. "The great thing, the essential thing, for a producer is to create *illusion* and *effect*," he insisted. "The supreme object in all my work has been to get near to nature; to make my atmosphere as real as possible, when I am dealing with a drama or comedy of life. . . . How can I expect to hold the attention of my audience unless I show them a scene that looks real? They see it, recognize it, accept it, and then if the actors do their part, the audience forgets that it is not looking into a real place."[29] This statement reflects one of Belasco's most important principles as a theatre man.

Belasco's productions were at all times characterized by the most exact and detailed concern with the small as well as the large facets of reality in a performance. Every feature in his productions not only resembled but *was* that which it seemed to be, down to the smallest detail. In his mature period he never allowed the use of a set which consisted simply of conventional canvas flats stretched out on wooden frames. Everything had to be real. Nothing, in his opinion, was as destructive to illusion or as ridiculous as the old-fashioned sets with flapping and shaking forests, parlors, and the like, which creaked and groaned whenever anyone moved about in them.[30] Both countless photographs and enthusiastic reviews of his productions testify to the fact that his settings appeared like marvels of solid walls and authentic accessories. "The stage director must be able to make his stage pictures live and breathe, just as a dramatist does with his characters," Belasco declared. "A correct stage setting is much more effective than the average manager knows. With the right effects in color, scenery, and costume the stage picture becomes as important a part of the play as are the actors."[31]

When it came to finding authentic materials for settings in his productions, Belasco's energy knew no bounds. For the extravaganza *Du Barry*, about Madame Pompadour's successor as the mistress of Louis XV, he spared no expense in importing authentic French drapes and furniture of the Louis XV period for his sets. In connection with this incredibly lavish production, performed in 1901 and requiring fifty-one speaking parts and 135 supernumeraries, no less than two complete books were published at the time.[32] Often months of detailed historical research preceded his work on such plays. This was the case with *The Darling of the Gods* from 1902, which takes place during a Japanese civil war and for which nearly all the furniture was imported from Japan, with *Adrea* from 1905, an adaptation of a classical legend set in the fifth century A.D., and with *Sweet Kitty Bellairs* from 1903, which takes place in eighteenth-century England.

It has become part of the legend surrounding naturalism in the theatre that when André Antoine produced *Old Heidelberg*, he bought the interior of a student's room in Heidelberg and transferred it intact to his stage. Similarly, for the *Théâtre Libre* performance of *Les Bouchers* in 1888, real sides of beef had proved to Antoine's audiences that they were, indeed, in a meat market. In the same vein, the climax of Belasco's photographic realism was reached in his fabled production of the otherwise negligible domestic drama, *The Governor's Lady*, in 1912. The play was written by Alice Bradley but, as was his custom, totally rewritten by Belasco in order to make it stage-worthy. On this occasion he actually reproduced on the stage for the play's epilogue one of the famous Childs' Restaurants in New York, complete to the last detail (see Fig. 3). Even the invigorating smell of the restaurant's celebrated pancakes could be sensed by the audience as they were prepared on stage![33] It was not without justification that Belasco ascribed the special quality of his productions to the care and emphasis which he accorded to the slightest detail. "It is as if he had taken the audience be-

tween the intermission, walked them around the corner of
Seventh Avenue, and seated them to one side of the Childs'
restaurant at that location and let the last act be played
there," wrote one amazed reviewer. "None other, save perhaps a Zola, could have held in his mind's eye its multitudinous detail or have had the art to translate that detail
into concrete terms."[34] Belasco's promptbook evokes in
full measure the atmosphere he established in this detailed
genre picture of New York life.[35] It is:

After eleven o'clock at night.

The interior in one of Childs' restaurants in New York
City. The restaurant is done in the usual white tiling.
The egg boiler, steaming coffee urn, steaming hot water
heater, wheat cake griddle, egg frying apparatus, etc.
are all in evidence. In fact, the place is exactly reproduced in every detail. The piles of oranges, apples,
grapefruit, etc. are arranged in the window. The pas-
try counter is well stacked, not forgetting the bowl of
doughnuts. Baked apples and prunes are set out. Thick
crockery dishes, cups, saucers, pitchers, small individual
platters, etc., are in evidence.

A lamp hangs over the Cashier's desk.

Hooks are placed at intervals on the wall for the hats
and coats of customers and signs are tacked up notify-
ing the guests to "Look out for your overcoat." Some of
the tables have a card "Reserved." Other tables are roped
off and stacked with chairs, showing that business is
virtually over and that although the place will be open
until midnight (this being Saturday) only a few stray
guests are expected owing to the weather. Some of the
lights are turned off.

Not only the interior but also striking details from the exterior contributed to the overall impression and mood:

> On the large window opening out onto the street, the sign "Open all Night" may be read. The window and doors show frost and snow. The heat of the room has melted the frost in spots on the upper part of the window and through these spots, snow is seen to fall and occasional flurries of snow indicate a strong wind. The pedestrians cannot be seen through the window; but it is evident that they are few and far between. Sawdust is sprinkled on the floor by the door. Occasionally the honk of an automobile is heard, and a passing trolley cable, with bell, etc. The arc light outside throws a strong light.

In Willard Mack's melodrama of the Canadian Northwest, *Tiger Rose* (1917), a forest was depicted on the stage. To lend this setting the proper atmosphere, Belasco sprinkled the stage floor with pine needles which, when the actors moved around on them, sent their odor out into the auditorium. In the second act of the same play a rain storm was presented with such convincing effect that the audience, upon going out for the intermission, was amazed (so runs the story) to discover that it was not raining outside the theatre.[36]

For the production of Francis Powers' *The First Born*, Belasco reproduced a glimpse of San Francisco's Chinatown down to its very smells. "Every pictorial accessory is right," testified the *New York Times* reviewer (October 10, 1897). "The senses of sight, hearing, and smell are violently appealed to for the sake of creating an illusion; for the perfume of Chinese punk fills the theatre and the music is as Chinese as possible." This production, the same critic added, was "the kind of thing Antoine, who has lately re-established himself in Paris with a theatre of the un-conventional, would eagerly take to." The comparison between Belasco and Antoine was one which was frequently drawn in the newspapers of the time. Not all reviewers were, however, equally taken with the special effects in this particular production. "The entertainment last night began with small whiffs of sickening, nauseating odor that was burned for atmospheric and not for seweristic reasons," snorted the *New York Journal* (October 6, 1897). "The theatre was bathed in this hideous tinkative odor of incense, and during the long overture, you sat there getting fainter and fainter."

While many of Belasco's performances attracted attention for their sensational theatricality, others appealed to audiences in plainer, more everyday terms. This is particularly true of the productions built around David Warfield, a former comedian with Weber and Fields' burlesque company whom Belasco made into one of the great popular stars of the day, an actor repeatedly rumored in the contemporary press to be the most highly paid performer in the world. David Warfield's power rested in his convincing personal projection of the attributes of warm, simple humanity coupled with humor and pathos. Among the salient features of his acting, Winter recorded, "were fidelity to minute details of appearance and demeanor and consistent and continuous preservation of the spirit of burlesque—a spirit which combines imperturbable gravity of aspect with apparently profound sincerity in preposterous situations and while delivering extravagant, ludicrous speeches."[37] Characteristically, critics compared Warfield's poignant portrayal of "simple-hearted affection, homely humor and sentimental pathos" to the acting of his great predecessor Joseph Jefferson.[38] In such productions as *The Auctioneer* (1901), *The Music Master* (1904), *A Grand Army Man* (1907), and *The Return of Peter Grimm* (1911) these qualities stood out against the background of an everyday, contemporary scenic milieu brought to life through a rich variety of verisimilar nuances. In *A Grand Army Man* one critic described "that wealth of atmosphere which, as Mr. Belasco builds it up, is in itself a kind of literature. The suggestive realism of Wes Bigelow's sitting room—a sort of visualized dramatic poem—the opening of the G.A.R. hall, the old courtroom, with its lifelike counsel and audience, merge into a picture real and American."[39] Long stretches of realistic stage business frequently enlivened these Warfield performances. In *The Auctioneer* a comic peak was reached in the first act when the title figure, Simon Levy, carefully deluges a pile of clothing in the auctioneer's shop loaded with all sorts of bric-a-brac with water from a watering can, then proceeds to smoke the clothes with a tinker's stove, and finally readies them for sale by marking the lot "Damaged by Fire"! Figure 4, from a photograph of the first act of Charles Klein's *The Music Master*, which deals with a musician in search of his lost daughter, provides another excellent illustration of the fully integrated, lifelike features of scenic environment which contributed to the effect of these Warfield productions. A completely realistic and intimate interior is depicted on stage, presented in minute detail ranging from the solid walls and three-dimensional furnishings to the real pictures on the wall and mantelpiece and the realistically set table. In the picture, dinner is about to begin and David Warfield as the host, Herr Anton von Barwig, is pouring the wine while his guests—napkins around their necks—stand ready to drink a toast. The moving pathos of Warfield's von Barwig made the role the most substantial success of the actor's career.

Countless other examples indicate the extent to which Belasco was prepared to put his naturalistic credo into practice, and put it into practice with resounding success for his theatre. In his steady hands things underwent a change, a magical transformation, so that it actually seemed to his audiences that they were witnessing an incarnation of veritable, living reality on the stage. "Look out for the details," Belasco repeated again and again throughout his career. "Let the big scenes take care of themselves. The little details are what count—what get over the footlights, what make people come the second and the third time to see the play. That's why I'm so particular to have all my properties correct. I don't try to have *papier maché* imitations made. I try to get the real thing. It costs more, but it is worth it. That's what makes the 'atmosphere,' the magnetism of the stage—the something the stage manager who is an artist breathes into his production."[40] The fact that Belasco never swerved from his conviction is amply confirmed by the contents of a puzzling and hitherto unnoticed promptbook dated 1931, the year of his death, and entitled *Virgin City*, a production he never lived to present.[41] In the wealth of notes and remarks here, one typically laconic and Belascoesque imperative stands out:

*Get time for dawn in winter in Nevada*

THE FAME ACHIEVED by Mister Dave, as many of his close friends called him, did not rest solely upon his minute

observation of realistic detail. His theatrical talent expressed itself in a special way through the unique atmosphere which he succeeded in bringing to his productions.
"The 'atmosphere' is the soul of the production," he asserted, "and no matter how beautiful the scene may be,
if it hasn't that soul it won't attract—it will be worth-
less."[42] Belasco had to an eminent degree the ability to
create atmosphere in the theatre, to imbue his productions
with an inner life. By means of strategically placed strokes
of realism he emphasized the atmosphere of a scene, increased its dramatic intensity, and even suggested abstrac-
tions.

Already during his early years in New York Belasco
won respect as a director for his ability to establish a particular mood in a performance. In *The Charity Ball* (1889)
he created the illusion of the tone and manner of everyday reality through an intricate pattern of lifelike details
woven into an atmospheric unity. The play is structured
around a strong situation in the third act, in which a
clergyman marries to his self-indulgent brother the girl
he has himself fallen in love with. The act takes place in
the sitting room of the rectory which, as a ground plan
in Belasco's promptbook indicates, was equipped in great
detail with a table, various chairs scattered about the room,
a settee, a piano, a bookcase containing books, and a practicable fireplace. This setting did not, however, serve
merely as a pleasantly realistic backdrop for the dialogue.
It was purposefully drawn into the action and used to
full effect by the actors. When the curtain rises, "a bright
fire is burning in a grate alcove and a sombre light re-
lieves the darkness of the room. The cold grey light of a
winter's night comes through the stained glass window,
L. at back." Having once established this basic atmos-

pheric tone, Belasco's direction quickly brings the environment to life through appropriate stage business and sound effects. "*Betts* [the church organist] enters folding doors L. He is carrying a candle. As he places candle on table and goes up into alcove *to stir up fire*, an auto siren scream from off R. at back, and a moment later *Bess* [sister of the two male principals] is heard off R.U.E." A few lines of conversation are exchanged between characters off stage, as Bess wishes them good-bye. An auto horn screeches and the sound of a motor is heard "until it dies out." On stage, the organist, who has been occupied with the fire, leaves the fireplace "at the same moment *Bess* enters R.U.E. There is snow on her coat and hat." Not until this point does the actual dialogue begin, with Bess's exclamation: "Oh Betts! B-r-r, what a night out!"[43]

In a scene such as this the purpose and effect of Belasco's method was to intensify reality by playing up the "real" stage environment—furniture, props, costumes, lighting, and sound effects—pictorially as well as dramatically. In his later productions, however, dramatic mood became more focussed and more specific. The stage context achieved greater complexity as it became richer in detail and, at the same time, more closely related to the characters in the play. Belasco's production books reflect clearly his growing concern as a naturalist with individualized concreteness and specificity. Those from his Lyceum years contain fewer and far less elaborate notes and stage directions than those from the period following his emergence as an independent producer, obviously with freer hands to pursue his own artistic purposes. The complexity and distinct individuality of environment in a play like *The Return of Peter Grimm* represent a sharp con-

trast to the comparative simplicity of the settings for
*The Charity Ball, The Wife, Lord Chumley,* or *Men and
Women,* all of which display basically similar traits of un-
individualized scenic realism.

William Bloch, Belasco's Scandinavian counterpart, succinctly defined the concept of specific atmosphere on the
stage: "When I walk into the auditorium at night, after
the curtain has gone up, the air, the atmosphere up on
the stage should make me feel the same as any guest walk-
ing into a strange parlor: the kind of house it is, the kind
of people there, and what goes on between them, before I
even step inside."[44] In just this way David Belasco came
to regard the creation of his stage environment. "After the
curtain had been raised upon the first act of *The Music
Master,* and the audience had been given time to look
about the room which was represented on the stage, the
main traits of the leading character had already been suggested before his first appearance on the scene," reported
the critic Clayton Hamilton. "The pictures and knick-
knacks on his mantelpiece told us, before we ever saw
him, what manner of man he was."[45] Belasco's stage settings involved extremely subtle selection. The living room
of the old Dutch house where the action of *The Return of
Peter Grimm* takes place was not characterized solely by
its solid, substantial reality. It was also designed to convey an atmosphere of memories, an atmosphere in harmony with the predominant nostalgic mood of the play.
"In the single setting for this . . . drama," wrote Walter
Prichard Eaton, "he carried realism about as far as it can
go and actually gave the sense not only of a room but of
an entire house which had been lived in for generations."[46]
The furniture was old-fashioned and cozy; bric-a-brac

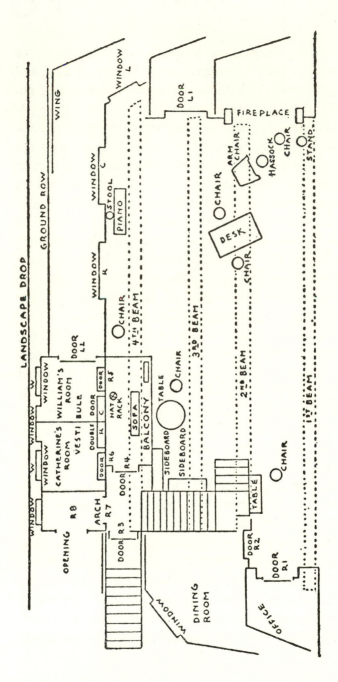

Ground plan, *The Return of Peter Grimm.*

was scattered around the room to project the intimate, homelike mood. An old fireplace, an old Dutch wall clock, and several fine paintings added to this impression, as did the rug on the floor and Peter Grimm's desk with a lamp hanging above it. Even the precise layout of unseen adjoining rooms is carefully documented in Belasco's highly particularized notes and included in his ground plan for the production, illustrated above. Notes from his promptbook further illustrate Belasco's naturalistic method: "The sun comes brightly into the room. Through the window can be seen tulip beds, other flowers, hot houses, and rows of trees. Peter Grimm's botanic gardens supply seeds, plants, shrubbery, and trees to the wholesale trade as well as retail; and the view should suggest the importance and extent of the industry which Peter has inherited and improved."[47] Hence character and environment were specifically interrelated. Each detail in the performance was shaped to make its individual contribution to the richly varied life and atmosphere of the integrated whole.

The device of drawing into the action the environmental components on the periphery of what is directly shown on stage is prominent in many other Belasco productions. In the Civil War drama *The Warrens of Virginia* (1907), he suggestively extended the atmospheric effect of the principal interior set by having a window in it open onto an adjoining hall. The audience was permitted to catch a glimpse of the stairs, a tall clock, the heads of people passing in this second room, thereby creating, in Walter Pritchard Eaton's words, "an overpowering suggestion of the spaciousness and solidity of the mansion." This and the other sets provided, according to the same critic, "eloquent proofs of [Belasco's] scenic power, a power that is not without its touch of poetry too, and never without the painter's taste."[48] Here as in many other productions, Belasco's vivid visual imagination added to the three dimensions of concrete, on-stage reality, supplementing them with a further poetic-pictorial vista of life beyond the set.

A major principle of Belasco's method as a naturalistic director was that no effect in a production should be used in isolation, for its own sake. All such effects were closely related to the play itself and constituted an integrated contribution to the clarification of its action or theme. "Only when the stage-director is resolved that the play shall stand first in importance in a theatre production can he safely employ the countless pictorial aids which contribute to its effect and appeal," he insisted.[49] Although famous for his lavish productions, extravaganza for its own sake held no interest for Belasco. His most dramatic and sophisticated stage effects were achieved with realistic touches that supported and emphasized the action of a play, placing the basic tone of a production in bold relief and contributing to the evocation of a particular atmosphere. "If for however brief a time scenery, accessories, or any of the details of the environment, no matter how clever they be in themselves, distract the audience's attention from the play proper or cease to be other than mere assisting agencies, their value is destroyed and they become more a hindrance than an aid and, consequently, an inartistic blunder."[50] Far from relying on mere literalism or facsimile realism, Belasco's methods, as his statement here suggests, were distinguished by the exercise of selectivity and suggestion.

For Belasco as for Strindberg, who in his preface to *Miss Julie* argues that suggestion increases the possibilities for creating illusion by giving the audience the incentive to conjecture, the employment of this device was a means of arousing the audience's phantasy. Already during his career in California, Belasco told William Winter, he realized that "it was not incumbent on me to show everything to the audience—only enough to stimulate the imagination"[51] because a much more powerful scenic effect could be secured in this manner. He adhered to this principle throughout his theatrical career.

Hence, in *The Girl I Left behind Me* (1893), Belasco was not satisfied in using ordinary photographic realism to depict the Army camp where the play takes place. Still more important for the theatrical impact in this production were its touches of suggestive realism. A military ball takes place on the same evening that a large and unexpected battle begins. Although it might have seemed effective to present this ball on the stage, Belasco resisted the impulse. The festivities were not seen, only the sounds of gaiety were heard in the background; meanwhile the stage pictured a small room where the soldiers arrived with their reports to the commander about the steadily mounting danger. Thus in this case a single aspect of the ball—the sound of music, laughter, and the gaiety of the dancers—was selected to suggest the whole. The result was an effective contrast between the off-stage festivity and the tension, seriousness, and mounting peril placed before the audience.

Sound, in this and numerous other instances, was one of the scenic values which Belasco integrated into a total naturalistic milieu. On some occasions, however, he did not hesitate to eliminate entirely an obvious naturalistic effect and thereby contradict his customary method if he found such a procedure to be justified. The production of Edward Knoblock's *Marie-Odile* in 1915 offers a good example. In a scene in this play, a group of singing soldiers are seated around a table in a convent which they have occupied. Their song is suddenly interrupted by the sergeant, who shouts: "Silence! Silence! Didn't you hear something? Listen! I—thought—I—heard—guns. Sh—! Don't you?" They listen intently until one of the soldiers who goes to the door confirms the fact that he too thinks he hears cannons in the distance.

In this episode Belasco did not wish that any actual sound should disrupt the play's subdued and grave atmosphere. His task, therefore, was to convince the theatre audience that they also heard cannons, despite the fact that this was in reality not the case. To achieve this objective he trained his actors at rehearsals to speak their lines over and over against the sound of a distant drum, which was intended to suggest the thunder of cannons. He persisted with this exercise until the actors were so accustomed to actually hearing the sound that, when the drum was eliminated, it continued to live on in their imagination. The imaginative power of this scene functioned so forcefully, he relates, that the phantasy of the audience was as strongly affected as that of the actors.[52]

DAVID BELASCO has provided a step by step description of his method in preparing a play for production.[53] He seldom followed the author's stage directions, preferring to arrange the staging personally so that the play's theatrical values were fully realized. His direction of Brieux's *L'Avocat*, produced in 1925 at Belasco's theatre as *The Accused*, offers a typical illustration of the principles which guided him in developing a *mise-en-scène*. On this occasion he collaborated with the adapter, playwright George Middleton, who was prepared to follow the sparse directions in the text to the letter.

When the curtain rises on the second act of this play, the audience knows that the attorney around whom the drama revolves has spent the entire night preparing a brief defending the woman he loves against a charge of murder. Middleton had simply intended to have the actor who played the title role, E. H. Sothern, wander back and forth across the stage to express his agitation. This expedient would hardly satisfy Belasco's conviction that a director "must *think in pictures*, so that each second of the play, from the rise of the curtain to the fall, may provide ceaseless occupation for the eye as well as the ear."[54] He immediately called for his prop man, Middleton recalled, a genius with the reputation of being able to produce a live elephant from his prop room if the necessity arose! Authentic French law books began suddenly to appear. Large strips of paper were torn dramatically into pieces and placed feverishly among the pages, indicating quotations which the attorney had found. A lamp remained lighted in the early morning sunlight. Drapes were partly opened and the French doors stood ajar to admit the morning air. As the final touch, a pillow on the sofa was crumpled to indicate where the tortured man's head had rested in a vain effort to relax. "This is how the room should look," declared Belasco. "Anyone can see now what he had been through."[55]

Another eyewitness has provided an enlightening account of how Belasco literally built a play during rehearsals. "The dialogue is cut, whole pages being ruthlessly blue-pencilled, because so much talk at this point impedes the action and spoils the intended effect. Or, possibly, the words so carefully set down in the repose and solitude of the study have a new sense to the ear in actual use. Or, again, this particular actor may not be able to bring out the value of the lines, and new expressions must be substituted which are better suited to his personality." Scenes were rehearsed in various ways to determine the most effective alternative. "You see a scene carefully gone over and over again one day," continues the account, "and the next you might not be able to identify it, though the words are perhaps the same you heard spoken yesterday. By a few bold changes the little scene has been transmuted into an incident fairly thrilling with spirit and animation."[56]

Belasco's sense for theatrical effect quite literally never miscarried, a fact confirmed by his countless successes. Yet his attitude toward scenic effect was generally shaped by a romantic viewpoint which co-existed with the naturalistic tenor of his art. The passion of Zola and Antoine for social criticism, for the depiction of raw and unembellished life, was usually absent from the work of their American counterpart. In his productions the most important function of milieu was as theatrically absorbing—not socially censorious—atmosphere. The purpose behind the minute care which he bestowed on every detail of a production was the interpretation and intensification of the tone of a particular play in order to engage the emotions of the audience as powerfully as possible. "The essence of success in a theatrical production, I have always believed, lies in its surprises," he remarked. "All lives have their moments of importance, and they are the thrills—the dynamic emotion. Why they happen, and how they come about is realistic drama."[57]

Both Belasco's own plays and his adaptations were saturated with the kind of unique, intensely picturesque, and romantic mood already alluded to, and it was this same evanescent quality of mood which he stressed in his stage direction. "The feeling of a scene is always a great factor in determining its arrangement," he argued, "for symbolism to a certain extent enters the production of every play."[58] It is possible to argue, as some have done, that Belasco in this respect operated with a conventionalized perception of stereotypes—*i.e.*, sunlit scenes indicate happiness, moonlight suggests a romantic mood, tragedy should be played in subdued light, and so on. It was not the case, however, that he worked in terms of stereotypes; his use of scenic effects, particularly lighting effects, was carefully tailored to the particular demands of an individual play. For Belasco, as for Stanislavski, there was no such thing as a feeling or a mood in general. A case in point is his perhaps apocryphal yet nonetheless characteristic exclamation during rehearsals for *The Darling of the Gods* that he did not want a mere moon—"I want a Japanese moon."[59]

In a perceptively formulated comment on the production style of Stanislavski, his former pupil, Vsevolod Meyerhold, draws attention to a feature basic to the theatre of Belasco as well. Meyerhold observes that the Moscow Art Theatre had what he terms two visages: the Naturalistic Theatre and the Theatre of Mood. The former, a naturalism derived from the German Meiningen players, had validity in reproducing nature as its basic principle. The latter, the more important style which eventually constituted the Moscow Art Theatre's real character, was evolved in the theatre of Chekhov which demonstrated the power of mood. The secret of this mood, in Meyerhold's opinion, was not to be found in the outer trappings of the performance but rather in its lyrical-mystical aspects, emerging from the special rhythm of Chekhov's characters and translated to the stage through "the extraordinary musicality of the performers who understood the rhythms of Chekhov's poetry and could veil his work in a lunar mist."[60] It was Belasco's misfortune—but not his fault—that he had no contemporary American dramatist of Chekhov's powers and stature to produce. Nevertheless, his theatre must be understood as a basically similar kind of theatre of mood and much lyricism. In Belasco's case, however, this lyricism did not depend primarily either on the text or the actors, but on his own extraordinary sensitivity to the poetry of light in the theatre, a poetry which in fact transcended realism and evolved a symbolic, evocative rhythm of its own.

## THE MAGIC OF LIGHT

DAVID BELASCO attributed the largest share of his success in the theatre to his sense of color as expressed through lighting effects. He felt that no other element in a production contributed as effectively as lighting to the projection of atmosphere and basic tone. "Lights are to a drama what music is to the lyrics of a song," he stated. "No other factor that enters into the production of a play is so effective in conveying its moods and feeling." And later: "To use color not for mere adornment, but to convey a message to the hearts of audiences, has become my creed."[61]

The function of light as described by Belasco in these sentences, as a means of creating atmosphere in the theatre, obviously goes as far back in time as the production of drama in indoor playhouses. Its magic and beauty constitute an essential element in the history of the perspective stage. The spell of enchantment evoked by candle lighting or Argand lamps or gas illumination, documented by countless witnesses to the progress of the theatre, has by no means been inferior to that created by the wonders of electric lighting on the stage. The lighting technique which electricity made possible, however, differed decisively from that which had gone before. Adolphe Appia is customarily credited as the first to have recognized and defined the infinite expressive possibilities contained in electric lighting. Appia was keenly aware that "light is the most important plastic medium on the stage," making possible "continually changing combinations of color and form, changing in relation to each other and also to the rest of the stage-setting" and thereby providing "opportunities for an infinite variety of plastic combinations"—opportunities which set the new techniques apart from the less flexible illumination previously provided by gas and calcium lights.[62] However, Belasco's practical experiments with all these factors of color, intensity, and distribution place him at the forefront of those pioneers who facilitated the realization in practice of the rich potentialities of electrical stage lighting. His intense preoccupation with these potentialities earned him the popular nickname, "the wizard of the switchboard."

Envisioning a comprehensive artistic unity as the fundamental demand of a performance, Belasco, like Appia, regarded light as the unifying principle which would link the actor and the stage setting in an artistic entity. In addition to the general illumination of a set in a realistically acceptable manner, Belasco's lighting always served a distinct purpose. In his view the lighting of a performance—its color, its stress, its comment—must be revealing in the fullest sense. Its function was to sketch and interpret the predominant mood, and to follow the pattern of development and interplay of emotion throughout a drama.

The interpretative skill and effectiveness of Belasco's

lighting techniques won him critical acclaim from the outset of his career in New York, notably in connection with
the plays he wrote in collaboration with De Mille. These
domestic dramas, staged with contemporary realism, were
visually accentuated and sculptured by means of contrasting shades and tones of color and light. *Men and Women*,
produced at the Twenty-Third Street Theatre, was played,
recorded the reviewer for the *New York Times* (October
26, 1890), "in the ruddy glow of sunset, in the dusk, in
the dark. Sometimes the scene is flooded with sunlight of
an excellent quality, and the moonlight has its accustomed
poetic charm." The pictorial quality of these effects suggests in some ways the mood panoramas of the earlier romantic theatre, bathed in atmospheric twilight, flooded
with sunset or sunrise, shrouded in ghostly moonlight or
the darkness of midnight. Belasco's exposure to the Californian theatre of his youth had opened his eyes to the
powerful potential of these older traditions, and their
presence can be felt in his later stage compositions. "Flickering lamplight, ruddy firelight, pale moonshine, and
brilliant, pervasive sunshine" predominated in the Lyceum
production of *The Charity Ball*, illuminating, according
to the *New York Times* (November 24, 1889), "the various pictures in such a way as to appropriately emphasize
the sentiment of the drama." Dramatic contrast, in terms
of color, intensity, and diffusion of light, was a Belasco
hallmark during this early period. In the first Belasco-De
Mille play, *The Wife*, the intimacy and tension of the
main scene, in which the wife of the title tells her husband
of her love for another man, were greatly intensified by
acting the scene in the subdued glow of the light from a
fireplace. "The audience follow it with breathless attention," the *New York Times* (November 4, 1887) recorded

enthusiastically, "with the strange feeling that, though deeply interested, they must be careful not to let their presence be known, for they are eavesdroppers. The spectators' vision," as naturalistic directors from Antoine to Stanislavski always hoped it would, "seems to actually penetrate the privacy of domestic life."

As Belasco's art deepened, finer and finer gradations of color and hue were used to interpret the shifting moods of a production with increasing subtlety and complexity. Set in a Californian mission, his own and R. W. Tully's *The Rose of the Rancho* (1906), an immensely successful play that ran for no fewer than 359 consecutive performances, endeavored to strike the basic note of languor and stifling, enervating heat. To accomplish this intention he continued for a long time to experiment with his lighting, without satisfactory results. He started by employing an intense white illumination which produced the right glare, but no impression of heat. It then occurred to him to cover the lights on stage with yellow silk and alter the color of the scenery to darker hues which would absorb the rays. In this manner he secured the effect of dry, hot sunlight, seeming actually to burn into the buildings on stage.[63] "Those who saw it," recalled Montrose Moses, "felt the drowsy vapor of the glow, the still air, and the enervating heat."[64] Belasco amplified this atmospheric impression of tropical heat still further by introducing into his stage picture at the opening a slumbering Spanish padre and his companion, a water girl half asleep, and two drowsy donkeys and their driver, who was seen deep in slumber in his cart! The sheer beauty of Belasco's light effects, whether for outdoor vistas, such as this one, or for indoor scenes, became proverbial. For *The Auctioneer*, we are told, he created "twilight in an old second-hand shop, just as eloquently beautiful as if it were falling in a rose garden."[65]

Because the basic principle behind Belasco's method of interpretative lighting involved constant, subtle changes expressive of the shifting moods of his productions, he did not operate with a static and unchanging lighting design. The general diffuse illumination of his stage was supplemented by a flexible system of movable spots and projectors. These movable light sources, counteracting the flattening effect produced by the normal footlights and borderlights, were used to achieve an atmospheric, plastic illumination of the scenery by means of constantly varying, delicately natural shades of brightness and shadow. Belasco also used sculptural lighting for the purpose of spotting and picking out an actor, emphasizing his importance, and throwing his figure into bold relief. Adjustment of the flexible lighting design took place through the regulation of one or more of the following three factors: (1) the diameter covered by the various spots and projectors lighting areas and figures on the stage, (2) the intensity and color scale of the lighting, and (3) the degree of movement. In the highly complex lighting design for *The Return of Peter Grimm*, for example, all three of these variable factors contributed significantly to the total effect. Moreover, this production offered an unusual opportunity for the imaginative use of the baby lens, one of the many technical innovations invented specifically for the Belasco Theatre by its gifted chief electrician Louis Hartmann. Hartmann regarded this device, a lens box housing an incandescent lamp with a concentrated filament, "the first decided innovation in modern stage lighting. It produced results radically different from those previously known."[66] Countless later directors who adopted these baby lenses frequently employed them as a kind of sculptural spotlight of obviously artificial origin. By contrast, Belasco's use of them produced a lifelike, plastic, yet essentially imperceptible effect, which in turn demanded a complicated balancing of these concentrated light sources with the overall stage illumination.

Through his lighting of *Peter Grimm*, Belasco solved a major problem of interpretation regarding the drama. He was keenly aware of the scenic difficulties involved in treating the physical presence of a spirit among mortals. Peter Grimm had to be in the same room with other people without, however, being visible to them. They were to sense his influence without seeing him. Yet Belasco wished to maintain his character free of anything "supernatural." Instead of relying on stereotyped eerie lights or fantastic makeup, then, he depicted Grimm in an entirely natural and normal manner, with only a differentiating light around him. In the production he seemed always to be moving about in shadow, while the other characters were always in a bright light. In reality, however, he was as well lighted as the others and every one of his facial expressions was clearly visible. The extremely detailed light plot from Belasco's production book presents the manner in which he accomplished his task: footlights were abolished and the faces of the other characters were illuminated with individual baby spots of a faint rosy hue while a cold, gray light was thrown on Peter Grimm's face. This imaginative use of suggestive realism projected the desired impression of Grimm, as a strong, returning, yet human force. Technically such a system of lighting also entailed the necessity of locating each character upon his entrance with an individual shaft of light, and then continuing to adjust to his movements about the stage without ever allowing the light surrounding him to spill over into the colder light which surrounded Grimm. In order to accomplish the mechanics of his lighting, Belasco equipped the unit set depicting Peter Grimm's living room with four ceiling beams (see plan, p. 70.) which helped to mask his lighting equipment. Louis Hartmann spent over a year perfecting the complex system of lamps used, and the gruelling, early-morning lighting rehearsals for the play are part of the legend of a production described by William Winter as "perhaps the most perfect example of stage lighting ever exhibited."[67]

One of the high points was, of course, Peter Grimm's second-act appearance as a spirit, a scene in which ultra-realistic lighting provided the major dramatic value. Tension was the dominant mood of the act. The director created the atmosphere of a cloudy, rainy afternoon whose visual gloom was reinforced by occasional peals of thunder. As clouds seemed to obscure the sun, the stage lights were momentarily lowered and the sound of rain increased; then, as the rain subsided, the lights came up again. Each time this effect of heightened, intensified reality (repeated several times by Belasco) recurred, the audience naturally expected Grimm's appearance. Shrewdly, however, the director eased this tension with a brief comic episode, during which the lights dimmed to indicate dusk coming on. At last the room was lit only by the warm reflection from a Belasco fireplace, around which everyone was gathered. Suspense again increased as one of the characters seemed

to hear someone entering and lighted a match, then another. But still nothing happened. Only when the maid
entered carrying a lighted lamp to dispel the gloom did
Peter Grimm make his long-awaited entrance. As she
entered downstage right, a spotlight from the overhead
bridge picked up her figure and drew all attention to her;
at that point Grimm appeared, quietly and inconspicu-
ously, upstage center, and was illuminated by his special
spotlight. Clayton Hamilton sums it up best: "As a fabric
for the theatre, it offered a very remarkable instance of
the technical triumph of the Drama of Illusion—one of
the most remarkable, in fact, that has been set before our
eyes in recent years. It conveyed with absolute concreteness an idea that was essentially abstract; and it succeeded
by a mastery of visualization, in convincing the spectator
that he was seeing the invisible."[68]

Many years later American theatre innovators of the
1920s appropriated this very system of plastic lighting as
an invention of their own. "Future historians will speak
of this period in theatrical history as the spotlight era," it
was then declared. "Indeed it is hardly too much to say
they have created our contemporary theatre idiom. . . .
Today our productions are characterized—conditioned
one might almost say—by conical shafts of colored electric
light. . . . We handle our spotlights and gelatines and
dimmers in the theatre with the same delight and the same
sense of mastery with which we drive a high-powered
automobile or pilot an aeroplane."[69] In the gushy enthusiasm over the wonders of the "New Stagecraft," the labor
which had previously been expended on the practical
realization of such wonders was lightly passed over, and
the adherents of the new movement conveniently forgot

the debt they owed to the theory and practice of David Belasco. Still later, a modern dramatist like Tennessee Williams, inadvertently repeating Belasco's own views on the subject, seems to imagine that an innovation is implied in his declaration: "Shafts of light are focused on selected areas of actors, sometimes in contradistinction to what is the apparent center. . . . A free imaginative use of light can be of enormous value in giving a mobile, plastic quality to plays of a more or less static nature."[70] Although Belasco would surely never have involved himself in producing plays "of a more or less static nature," these sentiments on the function of stage lighting might otherwise equally well have been his own.

Belasco was personally convinced that the aesthetic satisfaction which audiences derived from his productions was due as much to their manipulation of light, colors, and costumes as to the content of the plays themselves. In the production style which dominated his early years it had been the custom to intensify the emotional appeal of a given line or situation by means of musical accompaniment. Belasco felt that a far more powerful effect could be achieved, however, through the use of colors and lighting, which were better suited to the interpretation of the basic tone of a play.[71] For Belasco, as for Appia, lighting played the part of visual music, not only in the service of illusion but also of poetic vision. "By electricity the poetry of light is now made to picture on the stage thoughts not to be described—to realize impressions that mere words or scenes could not even suggest," he commented.[72]

This viewpoint was particularly marked in Belasco's *Madame Butterfly* (1900), which subsequently formed the basis for Puccini's celebrated opera.[73] One of the chief problems that faced Belasco in this production was the establishment of a transition from the opening, in which Cho-Cho-San makes preparations to receive her beloved Pinkerton, to the subsequent scene on the following morning. By means of the dialogue a mood of tension and expectation was established in the first sequence. Belasco wished to avoid the disruption of this mood inherent in a conventional curtain fall and a subsequent rise to reveal Butterfly's disappointment.

In the theatre his solution to the problem formed itself as follows: when in the evening the unhappy Butterfly sees the warship on which Pinkerton serves entering the harbor, she supposes he will come to her as soon as possible and becomes delirious with joy. She prepares to receive him, dresses herself and their small son (called Trouble!) in fine array, and fills the house with flowers and lighted lanterns. She then places herself, with the child and a serving girl, near the window to welcome him. There she remains, waiting and watching through the night, until the dawn breaks. The evening shadows darken into night. The stars become visible, brighten, then fade once more. The lighted lanterns go out, one by one. Finally the gray dawn reveals the servant and the child asleep on the floor, with the deserted Cho-Cho-San standing over them, pale and stiff after her long vigil. She continues to stare fixedly down the empty road as the rosy glow of sunrise brightens into full daylight, and the sound of birds singing in a grove of flowering cherry trees begins.[74]

The visual effect achieved here was not superimposed but served to intensify characterization, mood, and situation in the play. The fading light, the stars, the bird song emphasized the play's delicate, exotic atmosphere, underscoring the tragic note it strikes but also veiling its impact in the conciliatory glow which Belasco strove to impart to all his productions. The transition during which the light gradually changed from twilight to daybreak occupied an interval of several minutes (fourteen, claims Winter), during which no one moved or spoke. The basic device used to create this magical succession of visual impressions was as imaginative as it was simple. The *shoji* windows at the back of the Japanese room which was the setting, instead of being made of real, "authentic" paper, were done in semitransparent linen. Long bands of colored silk on rollers were passed slowly in front of an "olivette" (a powerful electric arc light in an open box, a device which Belasco subsequently came to regard as old-fashioned), thereby projecting diffuse, changing light onto these windows in a series of soft blends. The scene was so effective, wrote Winter, that "never did the interest of his audiences waver nor their attention flag."[75]

Belasco himself regarded *Madame Butterfly* as a milestone, "the first play to develop electricity in its use for stage effects, from the merely practical to the picturesque and poetical."[76] Significantly, the *New York Times* review (March 6, 1900) began in its first sentence by drawing attention to the visual picturesqueness of the production: "Beautiful to look at, first of all, is *Mme. Butterfly* . . . its brilliant display of color, its changing light effects, combine to make it a show that will be much talked about and that many persons will want to see." Clayton Hamilton viewed this performance as the unique realization of the visual potential of the modern theatre, which had reduced its dependence on purely literary elements and now expressed the poetry of the drama through the pictorial, visual resources of the stage. "It is by no means true that the drama has lost its capacity for expressing poetry," this critic declared. "It has merely altered its means of expressing it. David Belasco's original one-act version of *Madame Butterfly* was fully as poetic as the Elizabethan plays of Fletcher, whose verse still haunts our ears with melody as it echoes through the silence of three centuries."[77]

The production of Belasco's opulent Japanese romance, *The Darling of the Gods*, provides a similar example of integrated visual effects used in a symbolic manner to emphasize and intensify the basic motif of the play. This production can at the same time be seen as a typical expression of the many factors in Belasco's scenic technique which point ahead toward a more stylized utilization of theatrical devices.

A pantomimic-pictorial tableau, enhanced by a series of gradually changing lighting effects, established the basic tone from the outset. An exotic, flower-filled garden appeared behind transparent drops, producing a misty, distant impression. "It is late afternoon," reads the eloquent direction in Belasco's promptbook. "The sun is not far from setting. The shadows are long and dark, but between these it is still very sunshiny."[78] After a brief pantomimic scene which introduces the drama's heroine, Yo-San, the idyllic atmosphere dissolved. Following an "ominous peal of thunder" heard faintly in the distance, night began to fall and the stage gradually darkened. Soon, however, the darkness was punctuated by light. The flicker of a rose-colored lantern, then several more, revealed the dim, shadowy outlines of servants carrying lights. "The scene at first is in a faint mist," warns Belasco's note for this transition, "only a few lanterns shining out brightly, a soft blue moonlight coming up outside through the open shoji—which mistily shows the courtyard gardens—and stone steps and part of the palace in the distance." As servants lit more lanterns on the stage, others continued to carry in lights until the whole scene had become brilliantly illuminated.

Belasco's visually expressive evocation of mood through an intricate interplay of pantomime and the musically structured rhythm of light and color calls to mind experiments which were taking place in the European (especially the French) theatre of this period. During the decade preceding the production of *The Darling of the Gods*, pantomimic performances in such Parisian theatres as Felix Larcher's renowned *Le Cercle funambulesque* had created a veritable rage for this delicately suggestive scenic mode. During the same period, moreover, the ancient art of Chinese shadow plays had enjoyed a renaissance in Paris, particularly with the greatly admired *Les Ombres chinoise* of Henri Rivière that were performed in his miniature-scale theatre in the cabaret Chat-Noir on Montmartre. Both the evocative pantomimes and the exquisitely lighted dramatic fantasies seen in silhouette in these shadow plays reflected the growing preoccupation with symbolic suggestiveness, expressed through fleeting exotic colors and milieux, which absorbed progressive theatre practitioners around the turn of the century. Strindberg, Maeterlinck, Lugné-Poe, and others saw in the genre of shadow plays and pantomimes a viable alternative to the aesthetics of the traditional theatre, a means of reshaping and retheatricalizing the stage through the medium of mood and symbolism. Obviously, Belasco's oriental fairy-tale was never intended as an experiment in the spirit of the antinaturalistic avant-garde. Nevertheless, his production of *The Darling of the Gods* acquainted American audiences at a very early stage with the exoticism, symbolic pantomimic elements, and dreamlike, shadowy relief effects that were also seizing the imaginations of his more revolutionary-minded contemporaries on the Continent.

One of the climactic moments in *The Darling of the Gods*, which takes place during a Japanese civil war, is reached in a scene in which Yo-San is compelled, in order to save her lover, Kara, from the rack, to reveal the hiding place of his men. Belasco staged this scene in an "old sword room" with "lacquered walls and ceiling: dark, yet livid in aspect." However, the principal source of grim suspense and drama in this sequence remained its lighting effects. Belasco himself was of the opinion that he could have played it in its entirety only with the help of pantomime, and still not have lost any of its expressiveness.[79] At given intervals in the action, the doors to the dungeons beneath the floor were opened and the stage was bathed in the red glare from the torture chamber to which Kara was in danger of being sent. Without screams or groans of any sort, supported solely by the reflection from the torture flames, Belasco suggested to his audience a gripping vision of the dungeon's horrors and thereby motivated Yo-San's confession, which saves her lover from those horrors but betrays his men. In Victorien Sardou's *La Tosca*, containing, as critics of the day pointed out, a somewhat similar scene, the sense of horror was established by the agonized cries of the tortured victims. Belasco, on the other hand, worked skillfully upon his audiences' imagination in a considerably more subtle and suggestive manner. George Arliss, as the menacing Zakkuri, Minister of War, forced Blanche Bates, as Yo-San, merely to look down into the red glare of the pit and witness her lover's impending torture. "After thirty-three years," asserted Walter Prichard Eaton, "I can still see that blood-red light streaming up to gleam on the crafty face of Arliss, on the agonized countenance of Miss Bates. As a stage picture it was unforgettable."[80] The moment lives in the photograph reproduced in Figure 5.

A still more calculated effect was achieved toward the close of the same play, in a scene in which the surrounded Samurai warriors are compelled to commit ritual suicide together with Yo-San and her lover. Belasco placed this scene in a forest of bamboo trees "riven and burnt by lightning," behind which he depicted a large, blood-red, waning moon symbolic of the ebbing of life. He arranged for the setting to be painted in soft color nuances and to appear in deep shadow. His purpose was to cast the customary conciliatory mantle over events which might seem shocking to his audience, and at the same time to imbue the tragedy with its particular atmosphere. As the knife of Yo-San, the last one to die, is heard to drop, the moon disappears from sight, darkness envelops the stage, and all is silent.

The epilogue of *The Darling of the Gods* demonstrates in a similar way Belasco's remarkable ability to interpret and support mood in a visual manner. By means of visual devices, lighting, movement, and also accompanying music, the epilogue portrayed the symbolic reunion of the lovers. In an effort to suggest the ethereal and unreal quality of the situation, it was played behind a scrim lit from behind, thereby softening and obscuring the visual effect. The figures of Yo-San and Kara appeared surrounded by deep shadows, so that only their outlines could be perceived as they approached each other.

The stage directions for this episode in a realm where, in Winter's words from the *New York Tribune* (December 4, 1902), there is "neither trouble, nor parting, nor sorrow any more" are as follows: "Yo-San . . . is seen drifting up toward [Kara]. With shining faces and arms outstretched they meet. During this, music is heard: a slow crescendo to the point where they meet, when it swells into ecstacy, then dies, note by note. As they ascend to the next Celestial Heaven . . . the lights fade away, the curtain falls in darkness."[81]

Belasco has provided a vivid description of the manner in which he executed this scene in the theatre, a description which embodies a totally revolutionary technique both with respect to projection on to a transparency from behind and with respect to scenery painted in light. It appeared at first that nothing would come of his attempt to depict a kind of Japanese purgatory, "the River of the Souls," in which the bodies of the dead were to be seen floating skyward. He began by representing the clouds and the sky with conventional painted scenery, but it was soon apparent that this was unsatisfactory. In spite of every effort the girls whom he suspended in the air to represent the bodies of the dead persistently resembled very earthly chorus girls. "I could see nothing but the paint," he related. "Every time Yo-San ascended she reminded me of nothing so much as Little Eva in *Uncle Tom's Cabin*."[82] The illusion Belasco sought appeared impossible

93

to achieve. He ordered the set struck, and carpenters hoisted all the opaque setting away. As the scene shifters drew up the backdrop, however, a stage worker chanced to pass between a gauze curtain suspended at the front of the stage and a light at the back. Seen through the folds of the curtain his movements appeared almost ghostly. Belasco had the effect which he had been seeking. Aided by this felicitous accident he not only achieved a stunning theatrical effect, but also anticipated by more than a decade the widely used Linnebach lantern for projecting from the rear on to translucent screens.

In addition, Belasco decided to dispense entirely with painted scenery in this scene. Instead he surrounded the actors with white, unpainted canvas, securing the appropriate celestial blue color by projecting an intense white light through lenses covered by blue silk. This procedure, with its roots in the far-off days of San Francisco's Egyptian Hall, enabled Belasco to enhance still further the indefinite and distanced effect of his stage picture.[83] "For sheer, unearthly beauty," declared the critic for the *New York Sun* (December 4, 1902), "nothing in Doré's version of the 'Inferno' equals 'The River of Souls' with its plasticity of wave, its haunting lights, and the dim wraiths that flit through this Oriental Styx."

With a stage picture such as that described, in which Belasco achieved his impact through the use of color, light, and movement as tools with which to interpret the underlying symbolism of the drama for the audience, we encounter a theatrical style which fully corresponds to that espoused later by those intent on denying every connection with Belasco's name. An effect such as that created in *The Darling of the Gods* through the use of a lighted gauze transparency was subsequently appropriated by the American scene designers who considered themselves ultramodern and termed themselves pioneers of "the New Stagecraft," and was hailed as a "new" and revolutionary device for bringing to life the atmosphere of a play and imparting to it a special, poetic quality. In so doing these pioneers forgot the vision expressed by Belasco as early as 1903: "Fifty years hence will see a complete revolution. All the miracles that electricity has wrought, all that it may yet achieve, will be seized upon by the dramatist. . . . Electrical science will step in and paint his pictures for him. Sunsets, drifting clouds, sandstorms, flowing rivers— these and more, have been reproduced to the life. Who shall say to what ends this marvellous force may not be carried in its uses on the stage. Painted scenery, as we know it today, may become a thing of the past. The whole stage picture may be a light picture, and the scenic artist may yet be required to do with lights all that today he does with brushes and paints."[84]

In the productions discussed as well as in countless others, Belasco arrived through experimentation at many technical innovations having considerable future importance. There was no limit to the experiments, the expenditures, and the number of light rehearsals—the latter being a total novelty at this time—undertaken by him to achieve the correct atmospheric lighting of a production. Both of his theatres were equipped with the finest and the most elaborate lighting apparatus obtainable at the time, personally designed by Belasco in collaboration with Louis Hartmann. Both the first and the second Belasco theatre, the Stuyvesant, could boast a special lighting laboratory as well as the largest switchboard then in use in an American theatre. When the Belasco-Stuyvesant theatre was opened in 1907 the lamps in the footlights as well as those in each of the overhead border light strips were grouped in seven sections; each section was connected to a separate resistance so that any area of the stage or any figure or group could be illuminated individually and with varying intensities to create scenic mood. There were five strips of border lights with 270 lamps in each. Large or small "bunch lights" or spotlights, supplying illumination from a single source and imparting three-dimensionality, could be connected as required to eighty-eight connection pockets in the fly galleries and on the stage. The switchboard was equipped with a large battery of dimmers which placed lighting intensity under perfect control. Hartmann notes that in *Mima* (1928), Belasco's adaptation of Ferenc Molnar's *The Red Mill,* no fewer than forty-two dimmers were in operation; the light plot (of which Hartmann reprints a portion) filled fifty typewritten pages.[85] (This production was, incidentally, immense in other ways as well: the set was a gigantic machine made of tons of iron and sheet steel and incorporating 45,000 nickel upholstery nails to give the impression of rivet heads!) Merely these bald figures suggest the tremendous potentialities for the creation of a dynamic and plastic atmosphere inherent in Belasco's lighting plant.

His insatiable fascination with the power of stage lighting led him, moreover, into continual experimentation with new types and methods of illumination. Perhaps the most radical change he introduced in this respect was the elimination of footlights. Strindberg's familiar objections in the *Miss Julie* preface to the grotesque glare and unflattering shadows produced by conventional footlights were shared by many, not the least of whom was Adolphe Appia, who regarded these lights as a veritable monstrosity. It will be remembered that Belasco anticipated as early as 1879 the now accepted practice of front lighting as a substitute for footlights in his San Francisco production of *The Passion Play*. In 1889 he staged Sophocles' *Electra* at the Lyceum on a built-out thrust stage and completely eliminated footlights. For this interesting experiment in presentational staging he also tried to recapture the basic features of the ancient Greek theatre. An apron jutting into the auditorium was used by the Chorus, while the characters in the tragedy acted on an elevated portion of the stage toward the rear, backed by a facade of Grecian columns that permitted views of the countryside to the right and left. Because footlights were not employed, the Chorus appeared effectively in "Rembrandt-like shadow," while the rest of the stage behind it was brightly lit.[86]

Belasco continued in subsequent productions to experiment with the elimination of footlights (*Darling of the Gods, Peter Grimm*). One is therefore not surprised to discover Belasco's resentment toward the prophets of the New Stagecraft who tried to belittle and ignore his efforts and lighting innovations: "I think that we may fairly and without vanity claim to have revolutionized stage lighting. I confess that I have at times felt some annoyance when I have been informed by young writers in the press —who were not born until long after I had made great improvement in lighting—that in dispensing with footlights I have 'imitated' Mr. Granville Barker, Mr. Max Reinhardt, and various other so-called 'innovators.' Such statements are nonsensical."[87] Belasco's final step in this connection was taken in the season of 1914-1915 when he dispensed entirely with footlights in his own theatre. In their place a great iron hood was erected behind the pro-

scenium arch. This hood contained lights of varying power, and by means of reflectors the lighting was diffused
without casting shadows. To accommodate the need for
further supplementing and toning down, additional projectors were mounted along the side walls of the proscenium, though in 1917 these were discarded. Instead, a panel
about six feet long was introduced in front of the first
balcony which seemed ornamental when the curtain was
down, but which incorporated small shutters and projectors controlled from the main switchboard. These
sources in combination enabled Belasco to escape the unreal and shadowy effect created by conventional borders
and footlights, and to achieve instead an even and glare-
free light distribution which could be imperceptibly increased or dimmed at will. Belasco's changes and innovations in this regard "wrought something of a miracle,"
declares Kenneth Macgowan. "By such lighting sculpture
replaced the picture on the American stage." "In all the
theatres I visited at London and on the Continent," adds
J. G. Huneker, one of the period's most prominent critics,
in summary, "I saw nothing that had not been foreshadowed by the genius of Belasco; not the startling lighting effects of Gordon Craig, nor the atmospheric innovations of Reinhardt, nor the resonant decorations of Bakst
were novel to me, for I had watched the experiments at
the several Belasco theatres, had heard the discoverer himself discourse his theme."[88]


## DIRECTION AND ACTING

PHYSICAL, visual aspects of a production such as lighting
and stage setting were also regarded and utilized by David

Belasco as invaluable aids to the actor's art, aids which could be difficult to calculate beforehand and which therefore required extensive experimentation during rehearsals. The actor, in his opinion, was influenced psychologically by stage lighting, in a manner he perhaps was unable to explain. But he does react to the influence, and the audience in turn reacts to his performance. "I have sometimes doubled the persuasiveness of a speech," Belasco asserted, "not by changing a word written by the author or an intonation or gesture by the actor, but by increasing the value of the light in which the character stands."[89]

The methods used by Belasco in his direction of actors were decidedly autocratic. The press pictured him as a relentless monster who tyrannized over the hapless actors who fell into his clutches, bringing out the latent ability in them by sheer brute force. Belasco himself admitted, aware no doubt that he did not thereby diminish the aura surrounding his person, that he would "coax and cajole, or bulldoze and torment" his actors, according to the temperament with which he had to deal.[90] His unique personal capacity for developing and reinforcing the distinctive abilities of his actors constitutes a keystone of his theatrical success. It was no coincidence that his breakthrough as an independent producer occurred with the spectacular production of *The Heart of Maryland*, the propitious event which also established the first of his personally created stars, the fiery red-haired Mrs. Leslie Carter. Mrs. Carter, trained and coached by Belasco for two years and compared, when she acted *The Heart of Maryland* in London, to no less brilliant a luminary than Sarah Bernhardt, went on to display her tigerish temperament in such hits as *Zaza, DuBarry,* and *Adrea* before her elopement with an unknown young actor brought her volatile association with Mister Dave to an abrupt end. Similarly, other notable actresses tasted fame under Belasco's tutelage. Blanche Bates brought her talent for projecting vibrant, girlish innocence to such vehicles as *Madame Butterfly, The Darling of the Gods,* and *The Girl of the Golden West.* Frances Starr, an actress who shared some of Mrs. Carter's tempestuous emotionality, was seen in *The Rose of the Rancho, Marie-Odile,* and *The Easiest Way,* while the lovely, dark-eyed Lenore Ulrich starred in such plays from the later Belasco repertory as *Tiger Rose,* Molnar's *Mima,* and the record-breaking Belasco version of André Picard's comedy *Kiki.* Brightening the long list of other actresses who worked under Belasco for shorter periods are such legendary figures as Henrietta Crosman, the young Mary Pickford, Lillian Gish, Ina Claire, Judith Anderson, and Katharine Cornell. Among the actors the name of David Warfield remained linked with that of Belasco for nearly a quarter of a century, from his memorable portrayal of Simon Levi in *The Auctioneer* in 1901 to his retirement in 1924. The roster of other Belasco leading men is studded with such luminaries as E. H. Sothern, Maurice Barrymore, Lionel Barrymore, and George Arliss. During Belasco's final two decades in the New York theatre, Leo Ditrichstein, a playwright as well as a longtime member of the Belasco company, won acclaim for his acting in such productions as Herman Bahr's *The Concert* (in Ditrichstein's own adaptation) and Molnar's *The Phantom Rival,* while Lionel Atwill, a star of numerous Belasco productions, gave his best-remembered performance in 1920 as the famous French Pierrot in Sacha Guitry's *Deburau.* These and the many other actors with whom Belasco worked regarded him with deep respect and loyalty. They admired the passion for absolute perfection which characterized his work, and they realized the extent of their artistic debt to him. Even in his early years in New York, Belasco's renown as a director of actors reached formidable proportions. "This is the man," declared Alan Dale in the *New York Journal* (December 8, 1901), "who could rear a Bernhardt factory if he liked to start one, and who could do a big export trade in Irvings and Duses if he cared to advertize such an undertaking."

The nature of the illusion and effect Belasco strove to project through performance style in his productions was conditioned by the character of his repertoire and was generally typified by continually fluctuating and highly accentuated emotions. In performance style as in his productions as a whole, he chose at all times to emphasize the emotions which would aid in the creation of an exciting atmosphere—the intenser the better. A significant clue to an analysis of this style is to be found in his own statement: "The secret is that it is much easier to appeal to the hearts of audiences through their senses than through their intellects. People go to the play to have their emotions stirred."[91] Side by side with this principle, however, Belasco assiduously implanted in his actors the realization that the basic scenic atmosphere must stem from within, from the artistic and psychological consciousness of the performers.

The plays which Belasco performed were written or selected by him, as we have seen, for the sake of effective and dramatic situations, vivid and picturesque characters, dialogue having immediacy and sparkle. They were, in other words, chosen on the basis of their obvious suitability to the kind of theatrical style advocated by him. His conviction as a naturalistic director that life is a conglomerate of small details and that these very details must impart reality and atmosphere to a performance also found expression in his view of the actor's art. Through the medium of this art he sought to project a multitude of facets and reactions, a variety of sentiments, a succession of continually changing motivations, rather than one permanent through-line or attitude. "Remember in speaking that every sentence, sometimes every word, expresses a new thought or elaboration of thought," he admonished the budding actor to accept as a fundamental attribute of theatrical art.[92] This highly typical conception was repeated as an underlying prerequisite for naturalistic acting in other countries as well. Similar views are encountered again and again in the theory and practice of such directors as Stanislavski or Scandinavia's William Bloch. A cornerstone of the Stanislavski "system" of acting is his related technique of analyzing dramatic structure in terms of small units defined by the changing objectives of each of the characters.

Unfortunately, Belasco, unlike Stanislavski, never provided any truly systematic account of his ideas on the methodology underlying the art of acting. Many vague and generalized statements on aesthetics of acting and on the importance to an actor of such qualities as sensibility, imagination, industry, patience, and loyalty appeared from time to time in newspapers and periodicals throughout his career, but Belasco was never very specific about the relationship of his own working methods to these points.[93] As with other phases of theatre art, however, the key to

Belasco's approach to acting was a keen and unceasing observation of nature and humanity. Hence before the production of Lee Arthur and Charles Klein's *The Auctioneer*, David Warfield was sent out to study the population and local color in the Jewish East Side section of New York. "My trip included brief visits to the places from which are taken the various scenes and parts in *The Auctioneer*," the star related. "In the picturesque salesrooms I witnessed the bustle, chafing, and gentle humbug which marks auction rooms of every race, and at various places I saw the people from whom I have redrawn the characters for stage purposes."[94] In the year after Belasco's *The Auctioneer*—1902—Stanislavski and the members of the Moscow Art Theatre made their famous field trip to the underground haunts of the Khitrof Market, headquarters of thieves and outcasts in Moscow, to prepare for the production of Gorki's *The Lower Depths*. That excursion, like Warfield's, served, far more effectively than any discussion or abstract analysis could, to stimulate the artistic imagination. "Everything," Stanislavski records, "received a real basis and took its proper place." The subsequent work on the production "was guided by living memories and not by invention or guesswork."[95]

During Belasco's rehearsals observations such as the foregoing were brought into accord with the individual temperaments and personalities of the actors. They were utilized not in order to superimpose outward, stereotyped forms, but as a means of awakening individuality and stimulating the actor to live his part. Belasco's rehearsals were always keyed to the particular abilities of the artists with whom he was working. His directorial techniques were adapted entirely to the imaginative reactions which could be evoked from the individual actors. Significantly, he was much opposed to the customary and financially rewarding practice of organizing several companies of the same production to send on tour. "I have never directed a second company," he noted; "if I did, I fear I would change all the business of the play, and possibly make alterations in the play itself. I would discover immediately that what one set of players could do most effectively in a certain manner, another set would have to do in a wholly different way, dependent upon the temperament, personality, and technical equipment of each. When actors attempt only to imitate a model, they become automatons and the artistic finish of both the play and its performance is consequently sacrificed."[96]

Never proceeding on the basis of a rigid, unchangeable plan, the finished totality of a Belasco performance grew out of work and experimentation with his actors, to whom he regarded everything else in the theatre subordinate. During preparations for *The Music Master*, for example, sweeping changes were made to ensure that external details such as scene changes and special effects did not interfere with or detract from David Warfield's moving portrayal of Anton von Barwig. A series of tableaux, reminiscent of the familiar nineteenth-century technique so memorable in Irving's performance of Leopold Lewis's *The Bells*, was to depict scenes in which the music master dreamed of his past. In the dark, a double took Warfield's place in a chair on stage, while the latter actually moved through these flashback scenes. Realizing in the course of rehearsals that these elaborate tableaux detracted from the effect of Warfield's acting and jarred the tone of a production not otherwise geared to spectacle, however, Belasco ruthlessly discarded them. Instead, their purpose was accomplished mimically, in the simplest possible way, through Warfield's changing facial expressions, accompanied by a few occasional phrases as the music master sat musing about his life.

Another kind of challenge faced the director in the last act of this play. The setting was an atmospheric attic dominated by a skylight, its panes cracked and stuffed with cloth, allowing snow to sift in through the openings. "I liked the snowstorm very much, as it accentuated the misery of the characters grouped around a little stove," recalled Belasco. "Warfield did not like the storm, but he did not wish to say so; so he took a novel way to be rid of it. 'Brrr!' he said as he walked off the stage, 'I'm so cold! The snowstorm is so realistic it has given me a chill!'" Belasco's psychological sense did not fail him: he ordered a change in "the weather" immediately.[97]

Contemporary reviewers had the warmest praise for the quality and the psychologically motivated richness of detail which characterized the realistic acting style of Belasco productions. In addition to these reviews and to Belasco's own statements, moreover, pictorial records of the productions allow us to form a clear conception of the nature of this style. These production pictures illustrate a performance technique based squarely upon the highly accentuated emotionality that typified naturalistic acting as a whole in its first phase. During this phase many aspects of the earlier period's virtuoso star system with its boldly accentuated character portrayals created independently of an "interfering" director continued to live on in memory. Belasco, it will be remembered, had seen and admired in his youth such sovereign masters of the old school as Edwin Booth, Lawrence Barrett, John McCullough, Charlotte Cushman, and others. Throughout his life he continued to gravitate toward and to admire strong star performances in a production. As a director, however, it became his task to integrate such performances into a larger, naturalistic ensemble. One basic prerequisite for achieving such ensemble playing was extensive rehearsal. A carefully planned *mise-en-scène* and a prolonged rehearsal schedule constituted the two primary implements of the director's craft; through them he was enabled most effectively to impose his artistic interpretation on a production. As already noted Belasco generally scheduled a six-week rehearsal period for an average production. (Following a week of preliminary readings which concentrated upon details of role interpretation, and which were presided over by Belasco himself, he customarily turned the actors over to his stage manager, who supervised the initial rehearsal of the play on the stage. This practice, Belasco reasoned, created a certain sense of freedom in the individual performers, simply by compelling them to rely on their own inventiveness and initiative, while it also forced them to "squeeze themselves dry" before he resumed control for the remainder of the rehearsal period.) During this period a single will reigned. In contrast to the older practice of largely independent stars who tolerated little interference or outside advice, the naturalistic director dominated every aspect of the performance. In Belasco's theatre the major purpose of the *mise-en-scène* was to merge actors and stage picture in a single, harmonious unity.

The intensive energy he would expend on the creation

of performance unity became proverbial in his time. Re-calling the "long and arduous" rehearsals for *The Darling of the Gods*, George Arliss provides a first-hand glimpse of Belasco the director at work: "I would often watch Belasco with keen interest as he worked out a scene; some-times when he met difficulty he would suddenly stop the rehearsal and walk up and down the stage for as long as half an hour in absolute silence; but when he found the solution it was worth waiting for. He had really no idea of time . . . and sometimes he would go on till two or three in the morning."[98] Belasco's meticulous attention to detail naturally extended to the extras in his realistically indi-vidualized crowd scenes. When his army made its entrance in the spectacular *Heart of Maryland*, "each man in the line [was] individual and different from his comrade, both in make-up and uniform," asserted the critic for the *New York Dramatic Mirror* (March 28, 1896). "One has torn sleeves and a rough black beard, another has a whole uniform but a ragged hat and a scar over his right eye. A third is a sturdy old man with grey hair and clear-cut features. A fourth has muddy boots. A fifth with bright red hair carries his arm in a sling. And so on with the rest." Belasco's repertory in later years afforded him rich opportunities for the creation of yet more minutely indi-vidualized characterizations, even in the smallest parts. In *Zaza*, his adaptation of Pierre Berton and Charles Simon's French original, a divided box-set presented simultaneous action in the dressing room of the daring and wicked mu-sic-hall singer Zaza and that of the extras and chorus girls. Under Belasco's direction this set came to life and be-came an eloquent comment on a particular social milieu. "The men range from a doddering old rake to a boyish loafer, and the women from a besotted matron to a shy young debutante," observed the *New York Sun* (January 4, 1899). "All these characters are enacted as carefully as though they were to figure throughout the play instead of being merely incidental. They are distinct individuals, they behave naturally."

Belasco himself was acutely aware that the whole scheme of theatrical expression had undergone radical changes during his career, changes particularly manifest in the realm of acting style. The transition was not simply from the star system to a theatre of harmonious, integrated ensemble acting. Within this broad trend supplementary modifications occurred, tending toward a more subdued pattern of scenic expression, a less accentuated and heightened emotionality, and more "natural" and less animated stage movement and business. These widespread changes were again matched by corresponding shifts of emphasis and taste regarding the type of play presented. Moving away from the bright piling up of colors, images, and outbursts in the melodramas and extravaganzas which dominated the repertory of Belasco's early career, a progressive development led toward a less tempestuous notion of the nature of effective stage action and an increased concern with the minute reproduction of lifelike realities. "Stage traditions were good enough for a while till the audiences outgrew them," Belasco asserted. "One day the heroine who used to shout her grief till the gallery shook found no sympathy with her audiences. The acrobatic heaving of her bosom did not affect her audiences as they had in other years. What is the matter? Have they really grown tired of emotional acting? No . . . they had simply found out that there was nothing athletic in them. This sort of emo-

tional display became too unreal . . . so the ranting heroine
of melodrama was banished from the stage."[99]

The movement in the theatre of Belasco away from the
heavily accentuated and "athletic" expression of scenic
emotion and toward a relatively simpler and more subdued playing style went hand in hand with the gradual
de-emphasis of movement and physical actions on the
stage. Belasco's promptbooks from his early New York
period, particularly those for the Belasco-De Mille plays,
present a constantly varying pattern of blocking and business. Characters are called upon to emphasize dramatic
emotions in staccato fashion by perpetually changing positions, sitting down, standing up, retreating and advanc-
ing, turning around, crossing the stage, and so forth. At
the same time physical actions, in Stanislavski's sense of
utilizing stage objects for the purpose of endowing the
scene with an atmosphere of reality, related the actor to
the environment in which he found himself. Fires were
poked, curtains pulled, newspapers read, flowers arranged,
and dinners eaten throughout the performance. Belasco's
later promptbooks, however, indicate a gradually simplified and more relaxed pattern of stage movement and a far
more controlled use of business. An article titling him the
"wizard of the commonplace," in connection with the
opening of Pauline Phelps and Marion Short's play about
life in a small Indiana town, *A Grand Army Man* (1907),
elaborates on the natural impression created by these more
simplified and controlled staging methods: "There is not
one incident which bears the mark of having been introduced for dramatic effect. . . . No character crosses the
stage to sit or stand in a different place, merely because
the stage-manager believes that the audience 'wants the

scene broken up.' Of course such petty tricks are mere artifice, not art, and Belasco has banished them to the limbo of the 'has beens,' to join soliloquies and asides. People in real life are not constantly moving from one side of the room to the other. Why should they in plays?"[100]

The tendency to break up the dramatic flow with business was not peculiar to the naturalism of Belasco alone. Vladimir Nemirovitch-Danchenko and others have pointed out the early fascination of the Moscow Art Theatre with multitudinous touches of realism, particularly in productions of Chekhov. "One of the considerable elements in the scenic novelty of the *regisseur* Stanislavski lay precisely in this utilization of objects," Nemirovitch-Danchenko has observed. "In Russia this took place for the first time on the stage: the match and the lighted cigarette in the darkness, the powder in Arkadina's pocket, Sorin's plaid, a comb, studs, the washing of hands, the drinking of water in gulps, and so forth, *ad infinitum*." Like every innovator, the co-founder of the Moscow Art Theatre continues, Stanislavski fell into extremes: "Within a year, in *Uncle Vanya*, he would cover up the head against mosquitoes, would stress the chirp of the cricket behind the stove; for these effects theatrical criticism would go to great lengths to abuse the Art Theatre. Even Chekhov, half jesting, half in earnest, would say: 'In my next play I'll make the stipulation: The action takes place in a land which has neither mosquitoes nor crickets nor any other insects which hinder conversation between human beings.' "[101] Subsequently a reaction took place in the Moscow Art Theatre, just as it did in Belasco's theatre, against the exaggerated use of everyday, lifelife details, instituting a movement toward a simpler pattern of scenic expression.

Hence the atmosphere which Belasco strove to create in the direction of his mature productions was consciously oriented toward an elimination of unnecessary and distracting interruptions of the dramatic flow. Attention was focussed on a more harmonious balance between inner truth of character and outward depiction through business and movement. Arbitrary stage actions and "points" were minimized, "banished," as in *A Grand Army Man*, "to the limbo of the 'has beens.' " "We have gradually evolved into a liking for better things; we are always moving towards naturalism," Belasco was able to remark in 1911. "But we have never been able to throw off the delusion that so-called 'action' is a necessity. Very good actors of our time are seen pacing the floor of their drawingrooms, when entertaining their guests. They hop up and walk over to mantelpieces, lean on chairs, gaze into mirrors. . . . Such elements in acting should be done away with as much as possible," he emphasized. " 'Action' on the stage is wholly mental, and not at all physical."[102]

In 1919 he subsequently noted with satisfaction that "the excessive restlessness on the stage which prevailed a decade or so ago has given way to restfulness. . . . There is less sitting on tables, less crossing and recrossing the stage at regular intervals, less squatting on sofas, and less bouncing from chair to chair. The stage decorator shows himself to be most resourceful and efficient, and helps best the art of the theatre when he succeeds in preserving the tension and interest of a scene while his characters hardly move from their positions."[103]

In Belasco's case this transition to a more subdued and less abruptly accentuated pattern of *mise-en-scène* did not, however, lead to a direct de-emphasis of emotionality. It is indicative of his attitude toward acting that he repeatedly defended the position that "upon the stage it is never sufficient merely to indicate a meaning; there meaning must be conveyed. The art of acting is pre-eminently the art of expression."[104] Throughout his career he preserved, side by side with his naturalistic aims, this predilection for intense emotionalism reminiscent of the earlier ideals of the romantic period.

Belasco's preoccupation with pervasive naturalistic truth in every external detail of a performance was closely related to his idea that such authentic minutiae also served to buttress the actor's art. "My actors and actresses become letter-perfect in their parts when they forget they are acting and begin actually to live in their roles. How can they do this in an atmosphere of *papier mâché* and net and tinsel when it is as easy, even though more costly to surround them with reality?" he demanded. For Belasco the question was purely rhetorical. "If a play calls for a cardinal's ring to be worn by a player, I would far rather purchase an authentic antique than to provide the player with a cheap substitute. Why? Because in so doing I am clothing him in reality, not in pretense. That the audience may not see the difference does not enter into the matter at all. The point at issue is to give the player *every aid* to perfect interpretation of his role."[105] His fundamental aim of clothing the actors in reality in order to make them live on stage as extensions of an authentic milieu also demanded that they in turn absorbed, and were absorbed by, this milieu. Other naturalistic directors shared the same objective. Before the Moscow Art Theatre's elaborately planned production of Shakespeare's *Julius Caesar* in 1903, Stanislavski made his actors not only rehearse but also go around in the theatre in antique cloaks and togas in order to immerse them in the real experience of wearing period costumes. Similarly, almost from the beginning of preparations for *The Darling of the Gods* a year before, Belasco's cast rehearsed in Japanese shoes and kimonoes in order to become familiar with the costume.[106]

In the matter of casting Belasco preferred, true to his naturalistic aims, that the characters in a play should appear as realistically believable as possible. He carried this viewpoint so far that on given occasions he utilized French, English, or Italian actors in parts calling for these nationalities. "Ibsen should be represented by Norwegians or other north of Europe peoples, or at least by actors who either have or understand the northern temperament," he insisted, "for unless they have the 'atmosphere' none of the externals of stage settings can produce it."[107] *The Darling of the Gods* featured, in accordance with this theory, a partially Japanese cast, and *Marie-Odile* used a number of German actors.

Certain wholly nonnaturalistic factors were also present, meanwhile, in Belasco's selection of actors. Thus he pointed out: "If I happen to have selected an actor with a deep voice for a certain part, I try to put him opposite an actress who has a highly pitched voice, for when the talk floats across the footlights it must blend as in a song."[108] Belasco is in reality drawing attention here to the same factor which influenced his use of lighting effects: the utilization of all aspects of a production with a primarily atmospheric evocation in mind, an evocation in which transitions were of a consciously musical kind and were blended into a larger harmonious unity. This insight into the relationship of individual elements to one another in a theatrical performance as well as to the larger entity constituted the basis of his remarkable talent for theatrical persuasion. His method, often combining non-naturalistic considerations with purely naturalistic aims, produced a style which upon closer examination reveals many more points in common with the generation after Belasco than either part would then care to admit.

## OPPOSITION AND REACTION

IN THE STRUGGLE which gradually unfolded with increasing ferocity between the adherents of naturalism in the theatre and those who strained every effort to oppose it as diametrically as possible, Belasco stood as an uncomprehending figure. From his point of view naturalism represented the culmination of a centuries-long historical development. His opponents held a radically different viewpoint. For this reason both sides in the controversy regarded one another as equally great imposters—one of the milder appellations used in the debate.

The rallying cry for the new generation which emerged in the American theatre in the years around World War I was "simplification and stylization." "Truth in the theatre," declared one of the foremost champions of the New Stagecraft, Robert Edmond Jones, "stands beyond mere accuracy of fact. Unless life is turned into art on the stage it stops being alive and goes dead. So much for the realistic theatre. The artist should omit the details, the prose of nature, and give us only the spirit and splendor."[109]

For Belasco, who throughout his career in the theatre had expressed each of his intentions through the most careful selection of a variety of realistic details, a school which deliberately strove to neglect such details would necessarily appear not merely heretical but unartistic. "I am told," he remarked with sarcasm, "that art consists of pink and yellow and blue splotches of paint upon a curtain, or draperies illuminated from above by shafts of white electric light. I reply that when you use false lights and colors you do not stimulate imagination, you only distort reality. And when you distort reality you have destroyed truth."[110] The gulf between the new and the older theories of scenic art appeared too wide and deep for any form of bridge to span.

Yet many of the differences were more apparent than real. "We use light as we use words, to elucidate ideas and emotions," declared Jones—as had Belasco years before.[111] If one compares Belasco's staging of the transition scene in *Madame Butterfly*, with its symbolic use of lighting effects to emphasize and interpret mood and its dynamic interplay of natural light and shadow in a drama of their own, to a typically "modern" production from the American theatre of the 1920s—Maxwell Anderson's *Elizabeth the Queen* designed and lighted by Lee Simonson—it becomes strikingly apparent *how* small the difference often was in this respect between Belasco's approach and that of his successors. Lee Simonson himself chose to describe the closing scene of *Elizabeth the Queen* as a characteristic example of modern staging techniques: "During the final colloquy the light grew dimmer everywhere except in the small space where Essex and the Queen played their farewell. Just before they parted the blue of night through the windows began to fade to the pink of dawn. As Essex descended [through a forbiddingly lighted trapdoor to his death, recalling the moment from *The Darling of the Gods* shown in Figure 5], the added light vanished with him, leaving nothing more than a flickering candle. A faint tinge of cold blue light stole up the walls. The light through the slits of windows became brighter, almost red. And as Elizabeth straightened in her chair the first shaft of warm morning sunlight struck full upon her. . . ."[112]

Belasco's primary emphasis upon the evocation of atmosphere and mood through the integration of all aspects of a production was reiterated by proponents of the New Stagecraft in basically comparable terms. "A good scene, I repeat, is not a picture," proclaimed Robert Edmond Jones, "it is something conveyed as well: a feeling, an evocation. . . . It is a presence, a mood, a warm wind fanning the drama to flame."[113] "We have fought realism. We have berated Belasco," the champions of modernism liked to declare.[114] Indeed their revolutionary disgust with older traditions ranged far beyond the figure of Belasco. "In the middle of the fourth century [B.C.?]," asserted Norman Bel Geddes in the strident tones of the time, "the theatre went to sleep, simultaneously with the downfall of the Greek social system and the idealism of the Greeks. Ten years ago it rubbed its eyes!"[115] Despite repeated proclamations of this nature, however, it should be apparent even from the foregoing few observations that the New Stagecraft's professed opposition to the methods and techniques of David Belasco was not nearly so sharply delineated or so revolutionary as its adherents preferred to imagine.

In his counterattack on the new movement Belasco pointed to at least one factor which would subsequently, and with some justification, be used as an argument against this antinaturalistic trend in the theatre, namely the omnipotent position which the stage director came to occupy. One of the most prominent traits in the development away from naturalism has, of course, been the growing importance the person of the director has assumed in relation both to text and actors. These components were, at any rate in the case of consciously stylized productions, increasingly subordinated to the often highly individual interpretation and intentions of the director. Sharply opposed to this theatre of directorial absolutism, Belasco asserted that he had achieved his best scenic results by remaining in the background, inspiring and coordinating but never dominating. "The producer must be content," in his view, "to be only the unseen interpreter who directs the actors and, by the environment which he provides, creates the atmosphere which is in complete harmony with the essence and feeling of the play. On the other hand, in the fantastic productions of the impressionistic school of dramatic art, the producer is invariably an intruder in the play."[116]

It remained the aim and the vision of David Belasco to permit the spirit of naturalism to speak with its own voice, its own mood and atmosphere, in the theatre:

If, as I conceive it, the purpose of theatre be to hold the mirror up to nature, I know of no better place to obtain the effects of nature than to go to nature itself. To fulfill this purpose with integrity, to surround the mimic life of the character in drama with the natural aspects of life, to seek in light and color the same interpretative relation to spoken dialogue that music bears to the words of a song, is, I contend, the real art, the true art of the theatre. He who goes direct to nature for the effects he introduces on the stage can never be wrong. It is upon this creed that I base my faith in realism in dramatic art.[117]

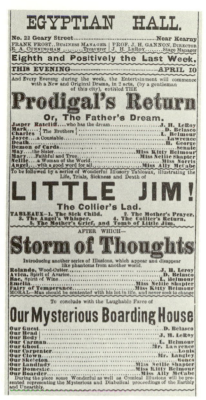

EGYPTIAN HALL.

No. 22 Geary Street...................................Near Kearny
FRANK FROST..Business Manager | PROF. J. H. GANNON, Director
R. A. Cunningham.........Treasurer | J. H. LeRoy........Stage Manager

**Eighth and Positively the Last Week,**

THIS EVENING...................................APRIL 10

And Every Evening during the week, the Entertainment will commence
with a New and Original Drama, in 2 acts, (by a gentleman
of this city), entitled THE

# Prodigal's Return
### Or, The Father's Dream.

Jasper Ratcliff....who has the dream.....................J. H. LeRoy
Mark...... } The Brothers {.............................D. Belasco
Charles................................................L. Belmour
Joyce...a Constable...................................Lawrence
Death...................................................B. George
Demon of Cards.........................................Senate
May....the Sister.................................Miss Kitty Belmour
Mary...Faithful and True..........................Miss Nellie Shapter
Nellie...a Woman of the World......................Miss Norris
Angel...with a good word for all...................Miss Ally McCabe
To be followed by a series of Wonderful Illusory Tableaux, illustrating the
Life, Trials, Sickness and Death of

# LITTLE JIM!
### The Collier's Lad.

TABLEAUX—1. The Sick Child.         2. The Mother's Prayer.
3. The Angel's Whisper.         4. The Collier's Return.
5. The Mother's Grief, and Tomb of Little Jim.

AFTER WHICH—

# Storm of Thoughts

Introducing another series of Illusions, which appear and disappear
like phantoms from another world.

Rolando, Wood-Cutter..................................J. H. LeRoy
Avica, Spirit of Avarice.............................D. Belasco
Rae, Spirit of Wine..................................L. Belmour
Emelia...........................................Miss Nellie Shapter
Fairy of Temperance...............................Miss Kitty Belmour
MORAL—Man should be contented with his lot in life, and never seek to change

To conclude with the Laughable Farce of

# Our Mysterious Boarding House

Our Guest...............................................D. Belasco
Our Head...............................................J. H. LeRoy
Our Body...............................................
Our Carman.............................................L. Belmour
Our Ghost............................................Mr. Lawrence
Our Carpenter..........................................Louis
Our Clown.............................................Mr. Langley
Our Skeleton...........................................Bones
Our Landlady......................................Miss Nellie Shapter
Our Domestic......................................Miss Kitty Belmour
Our Boarder........................................Miss Ally McCabe
During the piece some Wonderful as well as Comical Illusions will be pre-
sented representing the Mysterious and Diabolical proceedings of the Earthly
and Unearthly.

1. Playbill for the evening of April 10, 1877 at the Egyptian Hall, San Francisco. Belasco wrote all the plays named and also recited "Little Jim."

2. Percy Helton as little Willem, Tony Bevan as the Clown, and David Warfield as Peter Grimm in a first-act scene from *The Return of Peter Grimm* (1911).

3. Photograph of the Childs' Restaurant epilogue in *The Governor's Lady* (1912). Emma Dunn and Emmett Corrigan are seen as Mary and Daniel Slade.

4. Photograph of a first-act scene from *The Music Master* (1904), with David Warfield (left) as Herr Anton von Barwig.

5. George Arliss as Zakkuri and Blanche Bates as Yo-San in the fourth act of *The Darling of the Gods* (1902).

6. Henrietta Crosman as Kitty (left) and Katharine Florence as Julia Standish in their second-act encounter in *Sweet Kitty Bellairs* (1903).

7. Photograph of a later moment from the second act of *Sweet Kitty Bellairs*.

8. Kitty's expulsion from society in Act Three of *Sweet Kitty Bellairs*.

9. Henrietta Crosman in the fourth act of *Sweet Kitty Bellairs*.

10. The first-act saloon in *The Girl of the Golden West* (1905): Blanche Bates, as the title figure, tends bar, while the ominous gambler-sheriff Jack Rance, played by Frank Keenan, looks on, left.

11. "Oh, my California!" Blanche Bates as the Girl and Robert Hilliard as Dick Johnson in the final moment of *The Girl of the Golden West*.

12. Laura Murdock's tenement room in the second act of *The Easiest Way* (1909); in the photograph, Frances Starr is Laura and William Sampson is the seedy theatrical agent Jim Weston.

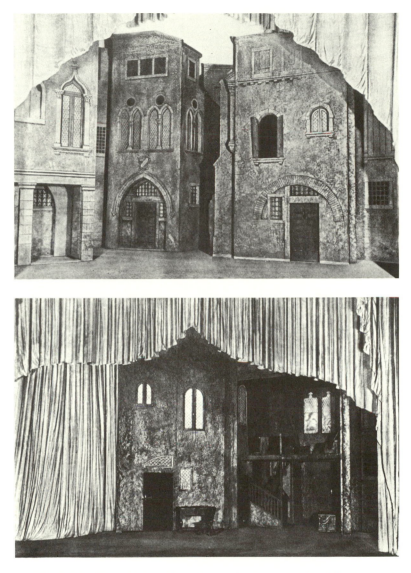

13. "Shylock's House" in Belasco's production of *The Merchant of Venice* (1922).

14. "Interior of Shylock's House" in *The Merchant of Venice.*

15. "The Casket Chamber at Belmont" in *The Merchant of Venice*.
16. "The Trial Scene" in *The Merchant of Venice*.

## CHAPTER FOUR

# Costume Plays of Manners and Customs: "Sweet Kitty Bellairs"

THE PRECEDING CROSS SECTION of aims and influences, methods and techniques inherent in the scenic art of David Belasco provides a theoretical foundation upon which one is better able to reconstruct, in a meaningful and fuller manner, certain of the key productions most representative of his art. At least four faces of Belasco's theatrical style may be distinguished, corresponding, as we have seen, to the categories of plays which he presented. A perennially hardy and successful category in his repertoire comprised what he himself liked to call "costume plays of manners and customs," productions which featured richly furnished depictions of exotic cultures (*Darling of the Gods, Madame Butterfly*) and historical periods (*Du Barry, Sweet Kitty Bellairs*). These period pieces were supplemented by a second group of distinctly American frontier dramas, among which *The Girl of the Golden West* stands out today as perhaps Belasco's most popularly familiar play. Less well known but equally significant in their way are the plays belonging to a third category in the theatre of Belasco, realistic social dramas like Eugene Walter's scandalous success, *The Easiest Way*. Finally, a fourth "face" of Belasco's style is represented by his single essay in Shakespearean production, *The Merchant of Venice*.

In all these instances, including the last, the style and form of theatrical production, rather than literary aspects of the plays presented, must engage our attention. Infinitely helpful in re-creating this production style as it appeared in practice is the rich mine of source material pertaining to each of the four productions selected for closer analysis. In each case, Belasco's own promptbook, in manuscript or in an authorized or privately printed edition, serves as the primary guide to his intentions. The reliability to be expected of such a guide emerges from the glowing words of Beerbohm Tree who, having produced *The Darling of the Gods* in London on the basis of Belasco's personal promptbook, declared to his audience: "Never in all my career have I received from anybody such a perfect 'script' of a play. Every detail, every bit of costume, every piece of business, every light, is set down for us, and every note of music furnished, making it all so easy to produce this play that we can only claim credit for carrying out his instructions."[1]

ANSWERING IN EVERY RESPECT to this description is the promptbook manuscript for David Belasco's *Sweet Kitty Bellairs*,[2] which opened on December 9, 1903, and went on to become one of the most successful and certainly the most characteristic of his historical period pieces. Supplementing this promptbook is a unique scrapbook of production photographs visualizing each important moment throughout the sequence of the action; from this vast wealth of pictorial material four examples have been chosen for inclusion here (Figs. 6-9).

Pictures, promptbook, and press reviews all testify to the lavish splendor of *Sweet Kitty Bellairs*. Freely adapted by Belasco from an undistinguished novel by Egerton and Agnes Castle, entitled *The Bath Comedy*, this romantic comedy of intrigue afforded ample opportunity for opulent authenticity in the scenic realization of its eighteenth-century Georgian milieu. With a production expense of $65,000, no small sum in 1903, a year Belasco found to be "the worst financially the theatres ever experienced,"[3] he followed the proven pattern of his earlier "period" performances. To provide the outward authenticity of detail which had already become a Belasco trademark he "sent an agent to Bath, England, to buy all the principal properties for *Sweet Kitty Bellairs*."[4] The resultant fragile charm and atmosphere of his historical milieu were achieved, according to the reviewer for the *Commercial Advertiser* (December 10, 1903), "with unexpected restraint and dexterity." Referring to previous productions in the same category this critic remarked: "In *Du Barry* and *The Darling of the Gods* Mr. Belasco has had his successes of enthusiasm. In *Sweet Kitty Bellairs*, which was acted last night for the first time at his theatre, he seems more likely to have his success of esteem."

In addition to the lavish physical production, a large portion of this "success of esteem" was due to the performance of Belasco's newly acquired star, Henrietta Crosman, in the title role. Aptly subtitled "A Comedy of the *Heart* in Four Acts," the central purpose of the play, as

William Winter observed, "is the display of a study in womanhood, an exceptional female character, a peculiar and fascinating type; and the predominant attribute of it, accordingly, is sexuality." Kitty is a woman of ravishing, sensuous beauty and reckless behavior, a merry widow in old Bath in the days of George III, "whose whole occupation is the bewitchment of man; and, in a silver fabric of gossamer comedy, this siren and all her associates are engaged in adjusting their amatory relations."[5] Hence Belasco fixed the dramatic focus of attention sharply on the personality and the performance of Henrietta Crosman— causing one German critic to speak with astonishment of the virtuoso skill of the actress (*schauspielerischen Virtuosenkunst*).[6] "All the striking moments of the play center about her lithe and buoyant figure," wrote the *New York Times* reviewer (December 10, 1903), "all the best lines come from her amiable lips. She is worthy of them all, and more. . . . In a word, Mr. Belasco has skillfully contrived to run the gamut of her well-loved charms." Moreover, the shifting motivations, subdued passion, and highly charged restraint of Henrietta Crosman's Kitty exemplify the combination of realism and strong emotionalism for which Belasco strove in his work with his actors. "Her coquetry had archness and innuendo, yet it never hid the good heart and the frank good-nature below. Once or twice, for an instant, Kitty opened that heart to her lover, and the deeper feeling that sprang out was not beyond Miss Crosman's powers," observed the *Commercial Advertiser*. "She could sacrifice herself for him with a half-hysterical thrust on her lips, and regret her lost happiness with no more than a resigned smile and a quiver in her voice. Throughout, her touch was light and charming, yet keen when the moment came, with nervous energy and suggestion."

The unifying, catalytic force which drew together these aspects of the production, meanwhile, fusing the performance of the star and her supporting cast into an effective ensemble and forging the realistic historical background into a functional environment for that ensemble, was provided by Belasco's direction. "A score of little details through the play . . . had individual yet harmonious effect," the *Commercial Advertiser* critic and others remarked. Each manipulation of setting, lighting, or blocking was made with an eye to the integration of "total theatre." Belasco's copiously annotated promptbook presents a detailed map of the methods and techniques followed by him in his quest for that totality.

To emphasize the consciously artificial atmosphere of his eighteenth-century pastiche, Belasco opened *Sweet Kitty Bellairs* with a rhymed prologue, spoken, according to the *Commercial Advertiser*, "by a young woman out of a Gainsborough portrait with a dark stage behind" and striking "a note of the time and manners to which Mr. Belasco would carry back his audience." The promptbook notes that the house curtain rose, and an intermezzo began. "The tinkle of the Prompter's bell is heard and the 'period' curtain, used entirely for this play, is seen." A Master of Ceremonies appeared and, "bowing profoundly," announced that "Mistress Antoinette Walker will speak the Prologue." The prompter's bell rang again, and the center curtain was drawn aside. Miss Walker was discovered "standing on a two-step platform, a bunch of flowers at her feet. . . . She represents a typical little beauty of Bath in fine coquettish array." The prologue actually spoken in this somewhat contrived curtain-raiser was unremarkable but to the point:

> George the Third!
> Because our play is of his age,
> He would intrude upon our stage,

and so on. Belasco was a shrewd judge of contemporary taste, however, and the *New York Times* found that these verses were delivered "with such simplicity and fluttering grace as to be perhaps the purest gem of the evening."

The background behind the prologue speaker was, according to the prompt copy, "arranged after an old picture." William Winter provides more information about this background, observing that "the old English city of Bath is shown, in a beautiful picture, and therein is displayed a populous, animated scene, constructed to exhibit as a background the raiment, manners, morals, and pursuits of Bath society, in the butterfly days that Sheridan and Smollett have made immortal."[7] Also in several of his productions prior to *Sweet Kitty Bellairs*, Belasco had made comparable use of geographic panoramas and historical *tableaux vivants* in leading up to a play through the evocation of the appropriate mood and spirit. To provide a satisfactory Japanese atmosphere, he had preceded the performance of *Madame Butterfly* with a display of a series of curtains depicting a rice field, a garden, and other views suggestive of the drama's environment. Similarly, the production of *The Darling of the Gods* was introduced by a succession of *tableaux* "symbolical of the theme of the play. I called this silent picture 'The Chase and Death of the Butterfly,'" wrote the director, "and made it indicate what was to be the fate of the heroine. . . .

It led to an interior scene which I called 'The Feast of a Thousand Welcomes,' brilliantly illuminated by vari-colored lanterns, for now I was suggesting to my audiences the ceremonials and festivities of Japanese life."[8]

Having in a like manner suggested the "butterfly days" of eighteenth-century Bath in his prologue to *Sweet Kitty Bellairs*, Belasco was ready to move to the play proper. In comparison with some of the more spectacular Belasco performances, this production was physically uncomplicated and required a total of four sets:

### Act I

(Late afternoon). Prideaux Hall. Temporary quarters of the Officers of the 51st and their guests (The Inniskillings) during their stay in Bath. The regiment has a "Ladies Day."

### Act II

(Four o'clock in the morning). Lord Verney's Lodgings. "Love is an old, old game, as old as the devil, God save us!"

### Act III

The Regimental Ball of the 51st. In Prideaux Hall.

### Act IV

(Next morning at daybreak). The "Bear's Head" Inn, Bristol. "The Rocky Road to Dublin."

No detail which added to the impression of solidity or authenticity was overlooked, however, with the result that these four settings required considerable time to change. "The waits were almost as long as the acts," recorded Gustav Kobbe in the *Morning Telegraph* (December 10, 1903), "and the final curtain did not fall until nearly half an hour after midnight."[9] This fact is verified by the promptbook, which records the running time for the production as five hours and forty-three minutes!

The first act of *Sweet Kitty Bellairs*, which establishes the basic situation of tension between the sedate "ladies of the regiment" and the vivacious and outspoken Kitty, and the latter's love for Lord Verney, a young lieutenant of the 51st, takes place in the garden of Prideaux Hall, temporary headquarters of Colonel Villiers and his officers during their stay in Bath. "Best of all was the garden, in which the first act passes," recorded the *Commercial Advertiser*, "with its ivy-covered walls, marble seats, arbor, and grimy statues, box hedges, and the soft English sky and rolling woodland beyond." Belasco's painstaking attention to environmental detail in this setting is noteworthy and characteristic. "Behind a tall hedge well up[stage]—we see the entrance to Prideaux Hall—over terrace the imposing flight of steps in profile—through a clump of trees, we catch a glimpse of quaintly furnished room—a spinet, old paintings on the wall, chippendale, etc. There is a flag on the Hall which occasionally folds in the breeze." To indicate that soldiers were temporarily quartered here, Belasco emphasized "a military aspect in the trappings on the steps and about. Occasionally sentinels are seen to slowly pass and repass the door. Amidst all the gaiety of Act, the discipline of the barracks should be felt." The naturalistic preoccupation with specific place and exact time is never absent from Belasco's design. Hence the backdrop depicted a view of Bath, "the Crescent, and in the distance, the Bathwick meadows in the sunshine, dotted with tents of the 51st and the Inniskillings." As the curtain rose the Abbey chimes were "sounding a psalm tune, as though for the quarter of the hour—no hour struck until six o'clock."

Henrietta Crosman's important initial appearance was shrewdly underscored by her director through subtle changes in blocking, without any hint of an unrealistic, melodramatic "entrance." "All bow toward R. as though to Kitty, though she is not yet seen. Kitty appears with Col. Kimby McFiontan. The Officers back down toward R., as she appears at the opening in hedge." But, Belasco's instructions warned, "there must be no 'working up' in this entrance—it must come easily, naturally."

Individual reactions and motivations were always carefully planned for in Belasco's direction of group scenes. Thus in the foregoing instance he noted: "The young ladies are pleased to see her—it is only the older women who show animosity during the Act." This division was, of course, reinforced in the composition of the stage group. Later in the act, one of Kitty's typically "outspoken" replies—"innocence is still a pretty thing, and fine ladies' airs of virtue are but too often a cloak for . . . willing frailty!"—motivated a particularly felicitous example of the kind of structured, posed emotionality that characterized Belasco's crowd scenes: "Lady Bab starts and utters an exclamation to Sir Jasper, who is embarrassed. There is a sensation among those within hearing. Julia Standish is so astonished by Kitty's daring that she gasps—occasionally tracking away a tear and sniffing. Hon. Mrs. Beaufort and Mistress Bate-Coome hear and say 'Oh!' in pants with indrawn breath."

The theatrical *coup* of the first act seems to have been the moment in which the sedate and dull Lady Julia Standish is literally "transformed" before the eyes of the audience into a gay and vivacious coquette by the knowledgeable Kitty, who provides her pupil with a concentrated course of instruction in the art of regaining an indifferent husband's attention. "You've wearied him out! You've tired him," states Kitty bluntly. "Look at you!" Turning Julia's back to the audience, Kitty proceeded to pick out her long curls and let them kink up again; the extensive face-lifting continued, hidden from the audience, as Kitty talked. Julia's apron was snatched off, her hat was set straight, her hair was swept up, her cheeks were daubed with rouge, her eyes were pencilled. "And what is the good of a pretty taste in petticoats if the world's not to have a peep at it?" demanded Kitty of the dull girl, providing Belasco with the opportunity for a still more daring and spectacular effect (*anno* 1903): "Bus. of lifting up overdress into panniers. Julia looks down half timidly at her exposed petticoat. . . . Shows hint of stocking." The metamorphosis was completed by a few strategic costume alterations. After spraying Julia with perfume and picking out the ribbons on her sandals, Kitty turned up the reverse cuff of both sleeves, displaying another color, and achieved the same effect with the neck of the dress. Finally, Julia's feathers were given "a whisk forward"—"they project ravishingly"—and she was turned around to face the audience. "Julia has been completely transformed," notes the promptbook, "appearing almost another woman." In addition to being a charming reflection of the popular taste of the day, this colorful *coup de théâtre* represents a striking illustration of the carefully rehearsed and timed precision typical of Belasco's stage.

Amidst the gaiety of this act, however, the "discipline of the barracks" was to be felt in the directorial concept. Plastic values of light and sound were, as always, Belasco's principal tools in the creation of contrasting, juxtaposed moods. The coming of night in this act presents a perfect example of his use of these technical devices to suggest mood: "A bugle call. Sunset effect. The day is over. Exchange of sentries. In the distance are heard the beautiful grave sounds of the cavalry trumpets—*not bugles*—giving the retreat. This is followed by the sounds of the drums and fifes, also distant, giving likewise the retreat."

Another atmospheric tableau incorporating light, sound, and movement brought the act to a subdued close. "The song of 'Kathleen Na Hoolihan' has grown very faint. The spark of Owny's lantern shows among the tents [in the background], which lie in deeper shadow—disappears in tent and song dies away. Lights have appeared in tents in the meadows. Curtain." The tableau or picture effect indicated by this direction was, of course, a favorite element in nineteenth-century theatre, and is concisely defined by Mordecai Gorelik as "a striking pictorial effect including both actors and setting. The actors usually 'hold' the tableau for some moments without moving."[10] In the theatre of David Belasco, however, the motionless, frozen quality of the nineteenth-century "picture" was abandoned, as various examples have already indicated, in favor of a more fluid, naturally animated *tableau vivant*.

The second act of *Sweet Kitty Bellairs* takes place in the lodgings of Lord Verney, the modest young lieutenant of the 51st with whom Kitty is in love. To dissuade the man she loves from fighting a duel which she fears will prove fatal to him, the impulsive Kitty visits his rooms at four o'clock in the morning—a fact firmly implanted at the curtain rise by the tolling of the Abbey bell, the chiming of assorted clocks, and the calls of the town crier, "his staff sounding on the stones below."

Belasco bent every effort to make this interior as naturalistically lifelike as possible, and critics agreed that "Lord Verney's lodging looked as though a man were living among its mahogany, chintz, and wainscoting."[11] The promptbook description indicates clearly the familiar Belasco touch: "The house has been built for one of the old citizens of Bath and now has come down to high-class lodgings, but the handsome wainscoting doors, walls, and window casings remain. Deep window seats, high windows with dark curtains. The fireplace R. is massive and beautifully carved. All the wood-work and doors must have an air of solidity. The knobs, latches, fire-irons, coal scuttle, candlesticks, bellows and all brass, silver, etc., should be real of the period. . . . The furniture, drapings, and detail of this room must [also] be the real of the period." Moonlight streamed through the windows, "forming contrast to red glow of fire as their lights meet R.C." Outside the windows, the spires of Bath Abbey were seen mistily in the pale moonlight, which slowly faded into daybreak during the act.

The room was filled with a vast multitude of furniture pieces and authentic, practical props—oval miniatures, dressing cases, brushes, combs, candles, snuffers, and so forth. Its most prominent feature, however, was a curtained bed upstage left, an omnipresent talisman in in-

numerable Belasco productions. "Dear old Belascoan bedstead," remarked the *New York Times* reviewer. "The one
unvarying rule of the mere London or Parisian dramatist
is: No struggle, no drama. On West Forty-second Street
they know better. No bedstead, no drama, is their rule. At
the end of the bedstead scene the love story is all told."

This symbol of Belasco's contempt for conventionality
provided, in *Sweet Kitty Bellairs*, a curtained hiding place
for Kitty and Julia, who have both come to Verney's room
to avert a catastrophe their mischief has provoked, but are
nearly discovered there at the unladylike hour of four by
the officers of the 51st. The sequence in which Kitty en-
counters Julia in Verney's lodgings at dawn offers a telling illustration of Belasco's masterful utilization of coordinated lighting effects to strengthen dramatic action
and suspense. Peering out at the unidentified woman who
has just appeared, Kitty "blows out candle. . . . Takes a
newspaper from spinet and tip-toeing across, throws it on
the fire. . . . The woman has started to rap a second time
when the paper suddenly takes flame and blazes up, casting a bright light over the room. Julia, starting at flame,
raises her veil." Figure 6 provides a visual impression of
this realistic effect; the manner in which it was achieved
becomes clear from the promptbook light cue: "Fireplace
to amber and back to red, then slowly up blue and amber
foots. Blue full, amber 3/4." At this date Belasco had obviously not yet fully eliminated footlights from his lighting design.

In danger of being discovered by the officers of the regiment, including Julia's husband, Sir Jasper, who arrive
for a drinking bout, Kitty and Julia are compelled to take
refuge in the curtained bed. In a comic climax reminiscent

of the venerable technique of the Screen Scene, the drunk-
en officers eventually discovered the hiding place, dragged
the bed downstage center, and danced around it in a satyr-
ic revel. Shielding Julia and taking upon herself the implied disgrace, Kitty then emerged from her compromis-
ing position alone, to the delight and astonishment of the
men. The photograph reproduced in Figure 7, which corresponds fully to a ground plan in the promptbook, shows
with unusual clarity that combination of vivid, balanced
group composition (note the double focus on Kitty and
on the swordplay downstage left), emphatic mimic reaction (the consciously straight line of gaping officers stage
left), and three-dimensional solidity of setting by means of
which Belasco brought such a moment to life on his stage.

In the following act of *Sweet Kitty Bellairs*, the scandal
touched off by Kitty's misinterpreted presence in Verney's
bed is utilized by the envious and spiteful gossips of the
place to dethrone her at a grand regimental ball the next
evening from her position as the belle of Bath and to disgrace her publicly. To spare Verney the humiliation of
marrying a woman of "tainted" reputation, she pretends
that she has merely been flirting with him. In despair, her
lover departs for the Napoleonic wars. "This was the great
scene of the play," recorded the *Morning Telegraph*, "and
all its varying moods were reflected in Miss Crosman's
acting."

The physical milieu for this act was incomparably
staged. The scene depicted three rooms arranged and decorated for a ball—the ballroom itself was offstage left. No
flags or military emblems were used, and the full dress
of the officers served to convey the military impression. No
lackeys were seen during the act, their duties being car-

ried out by soldiers. The entire scene was brilliantly illuminated by candles, and gave, according to the promptbook, "the illusion of great depths above and of opening
into other rooms." A system of staircases and a gallery
enabled Belasco to employ effectively both levels and
planes in the colorful composition of his stage picture.
"Perhaps there are too many pillars and too much gallery to make the ballroom seem as spacious as it should,
but the whole effect of a passing and repassing company
of *individuals* and not 'supes,' of brocades and feathers,
red coats, and white breeches, and what Bath would have
called 'elegant festivity' is gained with unbroken illusion," declared the critic for the *Commercial Advertiser*.

As this observation suggests, heavy reliance was placed
throughout the act on the colorful costuming and lifelike
animation of the crowded stage. Belasco's promptbook
gives a vivid description of the stage picture as the ball
guests continued to arrive: "The picture is now very brilliant—women beautifully gowned, with jewels glistening
in their hair, on their throats, bodies, and shoe buckles,
are talking to the civilians who are 'exquisites' in their
dress, but the dominant color is the rose of the soldiers'
coats." The action progressed continually on two levels.
Officers and guests wrote their names on ivory tablets.
Ladies fanned. "The scene moves continually," noted the
director. "Groups form, break up, gallants bow, ladies
curtsey. During this the music has stopped and we have
heard the loud buzz of conversation, the laughter, etc."
Laughter and conversation were suddenly interrupted by
the announcement of a distinguished guest's arrival: "His
Lordship, the Bishop of Bath and Wells!" In a manner
appropriated much later by musical comedy successes, "the

guests on lower floor—on stairs—on landing—everywhere, bend in profound bows and curtsies—all are down at once."

Unlike the standard, conventionalized "ball scene" of nineteenth-century theatre, and differing also from other Belasco productions, such as *The Girl I Left behind Me*, in which the ball itself remained offstage, the regimental ball in *Sweet Kitty Bellairs* depended on carefully rehearsed and individualized mass scenes, balanced and contrasting visual groupings, and a precise ensemble of music, dialogue, and movement. "As a slight pause ensues, the babble of the rooms grows a trifle louder," reads a typical Belasco direction. "Bab's faint laughter is softly heard in room above. Mr. MacKellar is a dark figure in a group of dowagers in gallery. Waving fans are everywhere. Civilians are talking to ladies at far back, the gay-coated officers in the background of the room above. This forms a second picture. At head of stairs Mrs. Bate-Coome, Mistress Beaufort, and others of Lady Bab's clique, are seated—no men with them—nodding their heads in gossip." With this bright and animated composition forming the background, the dialogue itself, among the officers present in Verney's room the night before, continued on the forestage.

The entrance of an orderly bringing an urgent message of impending battle—a favorite effect with Belasco—was not presented as an abrupt, melodramatic contrast to the previous gaiety, but was skillfully incorporated as a darker tone in the brilliant and luminous picture of the dance in progress. "The dance has continued," notes the promptbook. "As the above [entrance] has worked in with the music, there had been only a moment's pause—just long enough to show the dusty orderly in the midst of the dainty belles who approach him. . . . Kitty keeps up a fusillade of light raillery to the Irish whenever she meets them in the figure. . . . To be fully worked out at rehearsal —all done under the music—*sotto voce.*"

The highpoint of this act was, of course, Kitty's disgrace at the hands of the "respectable" ladies of Bath after Julia proves too spineless to corroborate her story. This scene "provides the supreme moment of the comedy," observed Winter, "and, however much its probability may be questioned, no spectator of it, adequately acted, will for an instant doubt its theatrical effect. The preparations for it are made with extraordinary skill. The scenic adjuncts to it provided by Belasco were of royal opulence. It is fraught with emotional suspense; it is a sharp surprise, and it has the decisive potentiality of a dramatic act."[12] It is noteworthy that the impact of the moment described by Winter derived from a highly stylized and consciously non-realistic treatment of the process of Kitty's dismissal. A nightmarish and intentionally monotone composition of hypocritically indignant silk-and-satin respectability seems to have been Belasco's aim. "Ladies calling 'Begone' etc. come to top of stairs. Some lean over stair railing, some come a step or two down the stairs, all furious. Mrs. Bate-Coome shakes her finger at Kitty. It is a complete picture of a group of ladies so angry that they forget everything but their rage." This scene is illustrated by the production photo reproduced in Figure 8. After a moment, this composition of righteous indignation was juxtaposed with the comment implied in a ruffle of drums that signaled the end of the dance and summoned the troops to war.

The act closed in a riot of color and movement, saturated with Belasco's sheer exuberant theatricality and highlighted by his use of trick, multiple curtain falls. The soldiers literally prepare to march off to the Napoleonic wars, apparently leaving the infatuated and despairing hero, Lord Verney, behind. "The song swells, the applause increases. Colonel Villiers, at the head of his officers, starts down the stairs L. The ladies in the room are waving handkerchiefs and flowers as the curtain falls."

This, of course, would hardly suffice, and the curtain rose immediately again! The stage manager's note in the margin of the promptbook suggests the pitch:

Song.  Ring Curtain.  <u>Swell.</u>

The officers, having halted in a line at the door, appeared to be waiting for someone. As Verney reappeared, buckling on his sword, one of his companions stepped aside to allow him to fall into line. As they marched out amid fluttering handkerchiefs, thunderous applause, and a torrent of flowers, Verney turned to Kitty and kissed her hand. "The curtain falls on the moving picture," instructs the promptbook—but once again it rose. This time Kitty alone remained on the stage. "She sinks to her knees sobbing, her face on her arm on the small stand C. The singing and cheers are heard in the distance. Curtain."

"After the clock has struck twelve it must necessarily strike one," mused William Winter in his most typical manner. "There is no thirteen."[13] Following the theatrical and emotional highpoint just described, the final act of *Sweet Kitty Bellairs* inevitably seemed anticlimactic. The mood returned to one of subdued realism. The setting depicted the interior of a quaint old inn outside Bristol, furnished with tables, chairs, a curtained bench, a fireplace "casting a ghostly flickering light," a "typical English bar," and other appropriately naturalistic details. During this act, Kitty's name is cleared and she is reunited with Verney before he marches off with his regiment. As a stark contrast to the emotionality and exuberance which had gone before, Belasco here maintained a natural, quietly reserved tone. The estranged and misunderstanding lovers spoke "like real human beings," asserted the reviewer for the *Commercial Advertiser*, "because what they felt they couldn't say. This was Mr. Belasco's triumph of restraint."

This play, like many other of Belasco's productions, closed on a note of inconclusiveness and bitter-sweetness far different in character than the strident happy endings of conventional melodrama. Impressionistic elements such as lighting, pantomime, and natural details of color, texture, and weather played an infinitely greater part in Belasco's direction of such scenes than grandiloquent acting. Thus, when the regiment departed through a deftly managed Belascoan storm of wind and driving rain, Kitty was left alone in the inn. With a cry, as though unable to resist the impulse, she rushed "up to the window and throwing it open, looks off toward R. The light is now clearer. The skies are still dull. The wet green boughs of trees [are] occasionally seen outside the window as though the wind were bending them down." This moment, considered one of the most memorable in Henrietta Crosman's performance, is captured in the wonderful photograph shown in Figure 9.

The same mood of restrained pathos, presenting a dramatic contrast to the tenor of Kitty's character at the beginning of the play, was reinforced by these devices of suggestive realism in a characteristic curtain tableau ap-

pended to the fourth act, entitled "In the Pouring Rain."
"Music *pp*. We see the exterior of the inn, past which the
troops have now marched. The inn is in the background,
some few lights showing from within. A hedge is in the
foreground. A sheet of rain still falls. Kitty is behind the
hedge, waving her hand to the troops. Nothing on her
head—as though she had run out, acting on the impulse
of the moment. The music of drums and fifes grows more
and more *pp*. Curtain."

For an "antique moralist" or for a seeker after bottom-
less profundities who might not readily respond to the
"gorgeous spectacle" of *Sweet Kitty Bellairs* or the considerable charms of Miss Crosman, the indefatigable
William Winter had a ready and apt response: "Enough
to know, in gazing on that spectacle, that it dazzles his vision and that the story pleases his fancy. He sees a woman
to whom humdrum conventionality is intolerable; a
woman who is fearless alike of vindictive feminine spite
and insolent masculine tolerance; a woman who can be
magnanimous; a woman who is nothing if not brilliant:
and all this ought to content even a cynic."[14]

## CHAPTER FIVE

# American Frontier Drama: "The Girl of the Golden West"

THE PRODUCTION IN 1905 of the vivid frontier drama, *The Girl of the Golden West*, written and directed by David Belasco, represented a peak in Belasco's endeavors to present a suggestively picturesque as well as strikingly "real" stage milieu. This popular play subsequently acquired more permanent fame when it became the basis for the libretto of the first grand opera written on an American theme, Giacomo Puccini's *La Fanciulla del West*, which enjoyed a memorable world premiere at the Metropolitan Opera in 1910 under the baton of Arturo Toscanini, featuring Belasco as stage director, and starring a sensational cast headed by Enrico Caruso, Emmy Destinn, and Pasquale Amato. An American frontier environment was depicted on Belasco's stage in other productions, including *The Girl I Left behind Me, The Warrens of Virginia*, and *The Rose of the Rancho*, but none of these surpassed the picturesque realism hailed by critics and audiences in *The Girl of the Golden West*.

"My youth surged upon me while I worked," Belasco recalled, and his play grew out of memories and experiences from his past, the tall tales and taller adventures of the primitive, transient mining centers in California that he knew.[1] For outward visualization in the play, he called upon every technical resource of the theatre at his command. His whole attitude toward the theatre had been formed at a time when audiences looked to the stage for some form of vicarious romantic adventure, presented in the guise of stirring spectacle, atmospheric effects, and general scenic opulence. The romantic penchant for the picturesque, for the sublime and overpowering aspects of nature, and for the romance of commonplace events permeated *The Girl of the Golden West*, set in the fabled period of the California gold rush of 1849. Within the play's broadly romantic design, however, Belasco incorporated a multitude of realistic details—visual, aural, and behavioristic—in a meticulously integrated and illusionistic totality. "Considered technically," commented Winter, "*The Girl of the Golden West* was a genuine masterpiece of stagecraft,"[2] and it is in this respect that the production continues to deserve attention.

From the instant the curtain rose on *The Girl of the Golden West*, Belasco began to steep his drama in a special mood by means of visual and aural effects. As a prelude to the dialogue itself, he introduced two purely pictorial scenes, "merely a few lines and lights," in his own words, "to show the steep, snow-tipped Sierras, the trail, the silent California night, deep ravines, and cabins of the miners of '49 hid amongst the manzanitas and pines." His purpose was to represent "a little world by itself, drawn in a few crude strokes, to explain more than the author could tell in a thousand pages."[3]

Putting this conception into practice, Belasco raised the house curtain on a dark stage and dark auditorium. A few bars of music were played in the darkness, after which the lights came up slowly to reveal a panorama drop depicting Cloudy Mountain in the Sierra Nevadas, the setting in which the drama takes place. Perched on the mountain side was a primitive cabin, the home of the heroine, "The Girl," with a winding path leading up to it. Belasco's stage directions for color and lighting are, as usual, highly evocative: "It is night and the moon hangs low over the mountain peaks. The scene is flooded with moonlight, contrasting oddly with the cavernous shadows. The path to the cabin of The Girl is especially flooded and the light pours down from the mountain above to form this. The sky is very blue and cold. The snow gleams white on the highest peaks. Here and there pines, firs, and manzanita bushes show green. All is wild, savage, ominous. . . . One deep sheer ravine is suggested, the purple mists rising up from the bottom."[4] Both the cabin and the moon in this drop were transparencies lighted from behind.

Since the time of de Loutherbourg's Eidophusikon, romantic scene painters, conceiving of the theatre as a "living picture gallery," had excelled in depicting natural landscapes of this very kind and with these very techniques, expansive vistas presented in an atmospheric and convincingly illusionistic manner. The imposing ruggedness of wild mountain tops, further enhanced by lighting effects of blue moonlight, red sunshine, raging fires, or erupting volcanoes, held a fascination fully as strong for American scene designers of the romantic era as for their European counterparts.[5] Although this fascination had not quite abated in the American theatre in 1905, the massive projection of mood and color in the opening tableau of *The Girl of the Golden West* had a more deliberate purpose of introducing the elements of a specific environment.

When this first impression of the vague mists of night

on Cloudy Mountain, painted on the top portion of a vertical panorama roller, moved slowly up out of view, the audience was led "down" the mountain. As the panorama rolled, the clearer outlines of the exterior of the Polka Saloon came slowly into view, the dark mountainside now seen in the background. The saloon, in which the first act takes place, was on the outside a rough, pine-slabbed building, "not new, not old, but weather-beaten." Like the preceding picture of Cloudy Mountain, this next view was also created by means of a large transparency cut in the left side of the drop. Lighted from behind, the building appeared to be ablaze with lights which shone through the windows and poured through rough cracks in the door. A rudely painted sign, declaring "Polka Saloon," hung in front. The sign was illuminated by a powerful, glass-encased kerosene lamp with reflector which stood on a rough lumber post. On the opposite side of the drop from the saloon the other key aspect of the play's milieu was represented; "everything down R. should suggest mines," notes the script, "it is evidently there that the mines are located."

The conventional orchestra music which had accompanied the showing of the first picture stopped, and atmospheric music was given a new and more functional value than mere background accompaniment by being moved by Belasco onto the stage and into the setting itself. As the lights came up on the saloon, the strains of "Camptown Races" were heard inside, the singer accompanying himself on a concertina. The gambling motif suggested by the song—"Bet my money on a bobtail nag, / Somebody bet on the bay!"—was seconded by other sounds of distant shouting and the occasional rattle of poker chips, "as though a poker player had won a big pot and was taking in the chips." Through the use of sound and light it became clear that life in the Polka was in full swing. The sound effects were continued as the lights dimmed and the panorama drop was lifted into the flies, thereby linking the pictorial tableau to the first actual setting, the interior of the Polka Saloon. Through the saloon windows and through its back door, the audience could discern the same lamppost and kerosene lamp described in the foregoing.

The special technique by which Belasco in this way led slowly up to the opening of his first act has been likened to "what is today a characteristic 'pan down' of cinema technique."[6] More accurately, however, the proper historical context to which such a technique belongs is represented by the highly popular tradition of *tableaux vivants*, panoramas, dioramas, and melodrama spectaculars current in the earlier romantic theatre. The principle of amplifying the action of a play pictorially, by means of panoramic drops, had been used by Belasco early in his San Francisco period, when he staged the chase scene in *The Octoroon* in 1878. Here, Belasco later wrote to Winter, "I used a panorama, painted on several hundred yards of canvas, and I introduced drops, changing scenes in the twinkling of an eye, showing alternately and in quick succession, pursued and pursuer."[7] This approach might have been inspired by the sensational escape scenes in other popular Boucicault melodramas, including *Arrah-na-Pogue* (1864) and *The Shaughraun* (1875). In both plays a characteristically cinematic "cutting" technique is used; in the latter, "the scene moves—pivots on a point at the back. The prison moves off and shows the exterior of Tower with Conn [the Shaughraun] clinging to the wall, and Robert creeping through the orifice."[8] In any case, pictorial effects such as the changing panorama in *The Girl of the Golden West* were necessarily dispensable under more primitive road conditions; hence the printed promptbook notes that "in most of the stock companies the curtain was taken up on the interior of the Polka Saloon in the First Act, the First and Second Pictures being eliminated."

The setting for the first act of this play (Fig. 10) provides an outstanding example of authentically detailed Belasco realism. The walls of the saloon were constructed of rough pinewood with many knotholes in the boards. "These pine boards to be the real thing," emphasized the author-director, "and all doors, windows, properties, and accessories exactly such as would have been used in a Western saloon at this period." Upstage, facing the audience, a typical frontier bar with fancy glasses and liquors for "show" ranged on a wall shelf behind the counter stood beside the door. The specific nature of this milieu was suggested by a pair of scales at one end of the bar, used to weigh the miners' gold dust. Behind the bar Belasco required such documents of reality as a pail in which to wash glasses, water, small towels, and several cigar boxes, including one box of "dollar Havanas" held in reserve for special occasions. Each of these props was, moreover, actually used in an effort to make the environment a living component of the total performance rather than merely a lifeless background. Among other props that contributed to the distinctive tone of the scene as well as to the suspense of the ensuing action was a safe fashioned from an empty whiskey keg, "made in such a way that the top can be withdrawn without having any outward appearance that it is other than an ordinary whiskey keg. This is where the *Girl* and the *Boys* place their wealth for safe keeping." A sense of the primitive and the make-shift was emphasized in a myriad of additional touches: boxes and cans piled in a corner near the bar, sawdust on the floor, saddles, bridles, and ropes thrown carelessly in another corner, unpainted pine furniture, gaudy rustic curtains of bright calico before the windows, crude kerosene lamps. A stuffed grizzly bear beside the door, wearing a battered silk hat and holding a small parasol in its paw, presided with comic dignity over the restless scene.

Both the production photo in Figure 10 and the lighting design suggest the effective interplay of light and shadow which Belasco achieved through the skillful variation of color, intensity, and area focus. Below the bar, stage left, was a square opening leading to an adjoining dancehall from which a bright, amber light flooded the room, generated by two open light boxes which faced a reflective backing. Other sources of light in the saloon were linked to hanging lamps over the various tables, and were supplemented by a few candles. In addition, a contrasting orange glow was supplied by a blazing "fire" downstage right (from a gas and electric fire log) in an adobe fireplace, "a regular old-timer, genuine, the sheet-iron all dented in."

The picturesquely detailed milieu of this Western bar, advertized by a sign in gilt lettering on the rear wall as "A Real Home for the Boys," was kept alive throughout the act by continual vivid action, character interplay and movement, dance, sound, and music. The dramatic focus and pivot of the play's suspense was introduced pictorially at the very outset: a large poster in bold lettering, tacked to the wall behind the counter, promised a $5,000 reward for the capture of the notorious road agent Ramerrez. When this desperate gentleman, in the person of Dick

Johnson, the play's hero, subsequently arrives on the scene, he promptly captures the unwitting heart of the Girl, proprietress of the Polka Saloon. While the obvious suspense generated by the ominous arrival of this outlaw plays a significant role in *The Girl of the Golden West*, Belasco's directorial concept did not center upon a melodramatic exploitation of this suspense or of the sentimental love element. As a naturalistic theatre man his chief aim—and the objective in the production which continues to hold the interest of a historian of the theatre—was to paint a believable, many-faceted picture of a group of people in an environment and at a time with which he himself was thoroughly familiar. He did so in a story which to his mind was perfectly faithful to life: "Why, I know the period Forty-nine as I know my alphabet," he stated, "and there are many things in my *Girl of the Golden West* truer than many of the incidents in Bret Harte!"[9]

It was the pattern of realistically observed local color, in human behavior as well as in milieu, which, rhythmically blending details together in an atmospheric unity, lent Belasco's production its distinct character and tone. The thorough musicality and rhythmic integration of his California genre picture was remarked upon by several of the play's reviewers. "It is enough entertainment almost," wrote one critic, "merely taking in the details of his stage pictures; things constructed with all the care with which music is orchestrated, with now and then some detached figure—a pale-faced, snaky gambler smoking a cigar, a serio-comic hanger-on stuffing his mouth with food from the other men's lunch pails—balancing the whole, and so to say, accentuating the key like the musician's pedal-bass."[10] More specifically, however, three separate areas can be distinguished in which Belasco labored in this act to orchestrate the overall stage picture: (1) grouping and costuming, (2) music, and (3) lighting.

As the scene came to life, a group of miners were congregated in the saloon for the night. Some were seated at tables playing cards, others stood by watching, a third group clustered around the bar. The bartender entered from the adjacent dancehall and proceeded to light the candles on the various tables. The concertina player, whose music had bridged the transition from the opening panorama to the first act, finished his number, went to the bar for a drink, and then made his exit to the dancehall. First at this point were a few lines of dialogue exchanged at the faro table, accompanied by music starting in the dancehall and the shuffling of dancing feet. This "natural" method of allowing the dialogue and action to fade slowly into motion was obviously not a trait peculiar to Belasco alone, but constituted a procedure common to many naturalistic directors, from Antoine to Stanislavski to William Bloch, in mounting both classical and contemporary plays.

The saloon picture in Belasco's production was further individualized in the external appearance of the characters. His approach to stage costuming was as particularized and specific as his treatment of every other phase of a performance. He viewed costuming both as a constituent of the authentically detailed environment and as a means of individual characterization.

The characters in the Polka Saloon presented a distinctly varied appearance. Among the ordinary miners, wearing riding boots, trousers, and variously colored shirts and scarves, two in particular stood out. "Trinidad and Sonora have endeavored to 'dress up,' as they are both in love with the *Girl*," notes Belasco's instructions. "An effort should be made to dress these parts unlike the ordinary mining characters." The unctuous and unprincipled faro dealer, known as The Sidney Duck, was distinguished by wearing an "old suit of city clothes he has brought from Australia." A full-blooded Indian also present in the Polka was attired in "part Indian, part American dress." He wore moccasins, a brass watch, and "a number of Carnelian rings on his hands . . . and pin in his scarf. His jewelry is very bad imitation. His necktie is fierce red." The flashy bartender, Nick, wore his hair combed down in a cowlick over his forehead and sported "a gay necktie. In his shirt sleeves and old faded 'b'iled' shirt, his red flannel under-shirt show[s] below cuffs. He wears a lively velvet vest. Wears very high heels, with a 'Frisco' cut to his trousers."

The formidable figure of the gambler-sheriff, Jack Rance, stood out in stark contrast to the commoner deni-zens of the Polka, distinguished from their generally weather-beaten appearance not only by his elegant dress but also by his whitish, "almost feminine" hands and waxen complexion, set off by a very black moustache. "He wears the beaver hat of the times, and an immaculate suit of broadcloth. His boots are highly polished, long and narrow with high heels, his trousers strapped over them. He wears a white puffed shirt, with a diamond stud held by side chains, and a large diamond flashes on his hand. He smokes the Spanish cigaros." This colorful character is seen in Figure 10 together with his antagonist, Dick Johnson, who is leaning nonchalantly against the bar. The latter was dressed in riding boots and pants, and, like the miners, wore a shirt with a scarf at the neck. However, a promptbook direction notes, "his clothing is bought in fashionable Sacramento," emphasizing the fact that "he is the one man in the place who has the air of a gentle-man."

In addition to grouping and costuming, music and sound effects were skillfully integrated by Belasco in his orchestration of the total stage picture. The Western music and sounds which emanated from the adjacent dancehall throughout the act were realistically motivated in themselves, but were also incorporated as devices to strengthen the action taking place on stage. At Dick Johnson's initial entrance a cue indicates that "*music swells*" in the dancehall. During the ensuing scene between Johnson and the Girl, Minnie, changes in the musical instrumentation underscored the shifting moods in the dialogue. As they met each other for the first time, the mandolin in the dancehall orchestra, which also included a guitar and two violins, stopped while the guitar continued; in subsequently less tense moments the mandolin resumed. As Jack Rance, the gambler-sheriff, moved into the conversation, as Johnson realized that the Girl was actually the proprietress of the saloon he planned to rob, and as Rance ominously called on the miners to aid him in discovering the stranger's identity, the music was arranged to follow the changing pattern of emotions. When the mood again lightened, the Girl danced off with the gentleman bandit to the tune of a gay polka, greeted by loud shouts from those in the dancehall. (The moment remains musically memorable as the miners hum the tune they dance to in *La Fanciulla del West*.)

The use of music to create atmosphere in this act was not, however, restricted to the dancehall orchestra. Belasco also inserted a wandering minstrel into the action, a banjo player modeled on an actual local figure whom Belasco had known in his youth. "I introduced a character in memory of the 'Jake' Wallace of long ago," he told William Winter. "I gave him the same name, made him sing the same songs, and enter the poker saloon to be greeted in the same old hearty manner."[11] When negotiations began between Puccini and Belasco regarding the creation of an opera from *The Girl of the Golden West*, it was the typically Western songs of this local minstrel which initially awakened the composer's enthusiasm. Jake and his nostalgic song of home live on today in Puccini's score: "Che faranno i vecchi miei/ Là lontano, là lontano,/ Che faranno?"

The third factor contributing to the special mood of the scenes in the saloon was Belasco's realistic, carefully integrated lighting design. A highpoint in this respect came toward the close of the act, as the miners departed into the night to search for the outlaw. "Six of the *Men* pass from L. to R. in back of window. Three with lighted torches, two with lighted candle lights, and one with a lighted candle lantern, red." Shortly afterward the candles and then the lamps over the tables in the saloon were extinguished, and the footlights were dimmed to mark the change. As the Girl straightened up the bar and the windows were bolted for the night, the intimate scene with her and Dick Johnson was played in a romantic semi-darkness, in which the glowing ashes in the omnipresent Belasco fireplace provided an atmospheric accent.

Belasco's technical mastery of stage resources is nowhere more unsurpassed than in the second act of *The Girl of the Golden West*, the climax of which constitutes one of the more legendary examples of his all-embracing naturalism. The act takes place in the Girl's cabin, which was staged with the same meticulous attention to small but significant details as the saloon. Belasco's precisely formulated stage directions describing the primitive interior of this log cabin, which consisted of a single room with an overhead loft accessible by means of a ladder in the ceiling, occupy no fewer than five closely printed pages in his promptbook! Particularly remarkable, however, was the manner in which Belasco in this act played upon the wild, overwhelming natural forces of the exterior environment to augment and reinforce the dramatic action.

Earlier Belasco productions had, of course, incorporated astonishing natural phenomena. In Paul M. Potter's *Under Two Flags* (1901), in which Blanche Bates's passionate and patirotic Cigarette made her a star, a Belasco sandstorm, created by means of shadows thrown by a stereopticon upon a screen between the stage and the audience, astonished reviewers of the Moorish fantasy. "The wind sighs in the distance and rages as it comes near," recorded the *New York Sun* (February 10, 1901) in amazement. "The light of day fades to dimness. . . . Rapid reflections on gauze curtains, in conjunction with the noises of the wind and the bending of trees, made a really awe-inspiring imitation of a natural phenomenon."[12] All previous wizardry paled, however, in the face of the nature unleashed by Belasco in *The Girl of the Golden West*.

Despite the mounting danger that his identity as Ramerrez may be revealed at any moment in an area where he is being intensively hunted, Dick Johnson comes to Minnie's cabin. As they talk, totally engrossed in one another and oblivious to everything around them, a violent blizzard begins to take form, suggesting to the audience in a realistic manner the approach of danger. When the setting for the log cabin interior was first revealed, it disclosed dimly a distant view of rugged, snow-clad mountains, seen through the windows at the back. As a driving wind rose and the snowfall set in, this view gradually faded and the window casements became obscured by sleet. The curtains in the cabin were seen blowing, a small basket on a wardrobe was knocked off, a flower pot fell from its stand, and several pieces of white tissue paper were blown across the floor from a case under the bed. All of these effects were achieved by the use of wind machines and blowers stationed, as the ground plan (illustrated p. 153) indicates, behind the "Belascoan bedstead," in the wings, and in front of one of the upstage windows. The swirling snowfall that gradually obscured the view from the cabin windows required three rows of "snow bags" in the flies filled with salt as well as two boxes of rock salt for the sleet accumulation on the windows. Electric fans gave these elements an added swirling effect as they fell. Moreover, a gauze drop was lowered to soften and obscure the mountain drop visible through the windows and the door before the start of the blizzard. As the snow then "covered" the landscape, the original exterior backdrop was replaced by an "exterior snow drop," depicting a landscape identical to the first but now covered with snow. The "air tanks" which produced shrieks of wind and the cold blue tone with which Belasco lit his snowy landscape also contributed additional dimensions to the pictorial effect.

No richer description of the impact which this scene had on theatre audiences could be wished for than that provided by William Winter: "Throughout the progress of the action, intensifying the sense of desolation, dread, and terror, the audience heard the wild moaning and shrill whistle of the gale and, at the moments as the tempest rose to a climax of fury, could see the fine-powdered snow driven in tiny sprays and eddies through every crevice of the walls and the very fabric of the cabin quiver and rock beneath the impact of terrific blasts of wind—long

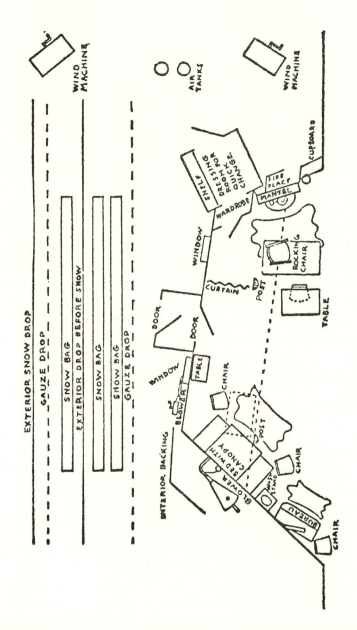

EXTERIOR SNOW DROP

GAUZE DROP

SNOW BAG

EXTERIOR DROP BEFORE SNOW

SNOW BAG

SNOW BAG

GAUZE DROP

WIND MACHINE

AIR TANKS

WIND MACHINE

CUPBOARD

FIRE PLACE

MANTEL

SHELF

DRESSING ROOM FOR QUICK CHANGE

WARDROBE

WINDOW

CURTAIN

POST

ROCKING CHAIR

TABLE

DOOR

DOOR

WINDOW

BLOWER

TABLE

CHAIR

POST

EXTERIOR BACKING

BLOWER

BED WITH CANOPY

HAND STAND

CHAIR

BUREAU

CHAIR

Ground plan, *The Girl of the Golden West*, Act II.

shrieking down the mountain sides before they struck—while in every fitful pause was audible the sharp click-click of freezing snow driving on wall and window." The operation of the necessary stage machinery for this scene required, Winter adds, a force of no less than thirty-two trained stagehands, "a sort of mechanical orchestra, directed by a centrally placed conductor who was visible from the special station of each worker."[13]

Dramatically, as Winter's description indicates, the snowstorm increased the audience's sensation of the danger and wildness of the milieu and the situation. It was not merely a clever exploitation on Belasco's part of the tricks and mechanics of the theatre. The dimension of suspense which it contributed to the dramatic action was not artificially imposed. It answered for Belasco the specific purpose of depicting dynamically the deterministic interaction of what Zola in his Preface to *Thérèse Raquin* had termed "the two-fold life of the character and its environment." It might be argued that Belasco's environment in this case virtually assumed the role of a dramatic antagonist.

The storm effects continued through the remainder of the act, but in a much lower and more subdued key. The action which now followed focused on the dramatic—or, if one prefers that dubious and imprecisely used term, "melodramatic"—suspense created by the two central characters. Belasco moved smoothly from a wide-angle depiction of natural fury to a close-up situation between his two stars, Blanche Bates and Robert Hilliard. Dick Johnson, whose true identity is now known by Minnie as well as the sheriff, is about to flee from the cabin. He is wounded, however, and stumbles back inside, where the Girl in desperation conceals him in the loft. The sheriff arrives, still unsuccessful in his manhunt. As he is about to go out again into the blizzard, a drop of blood suddenly falls from the rafters overhead, first on his hand and then on the handkerchief he is holding. "In the glare of the spotlight," wrote a contemporary critic of this stark moment, "the dark spot can be seen by every one in the audience. The sheriff slowly looks down, then up. He is tall and gaunt, all in black, face white as death. His gaze fixes itself on the rafters and then, in the silence, on the white handkerchief, drop—drop—drop falls the blood. The situation has the bite of theatrical genius."[14]

As this situation suggests, Belasco's directorial ability to charge a given moment with a theatricality that electrified audiences was by no means confined to external elements such as setting or lighting. This ability expressed itself with equal power in the illusion of intense and supreme "reality" that he created through his work with the behavior of his actors. His work in this respect parallels the methods of other naturalistic directors, most notably Stanislavski, quite closely. Belasco provided his actors with various physical tasks and specific kinds of business in order both to create believable characters with realistic patterns of behavior and to relate the characters to their milieu. For example, when Rance and others arrived to tell the Girl of Johnson's true identity, the director planned various physical actions for them: "Rance goes to table, back of it, warming his hands over candle; takes off gloves, brushes snow off with handkerchief onto floor, as do all the men." When the snow (actually salt) is brushed off into the fireplace, the fire—naturally—hisses. Later Rance, obviously still cold, spread "his stiffened fingers before the blaze." The weave of continual physical tasks extended to every character in the scene. The kind-hearted Sonora, who in the third act secures Johnson's release, "stamps feet. His nose is red—his ears and his hands, which he takes out of heavy fur mittens, are very red—he rubs them together." Later the same character could be seen "breathing on his fingers."

It is no coincidence that one of the aspects of the production which most impressed the reviewers was precisely this rich pattern of stage business. Arthur Ruhl singled out the performance of Frank Keenan as Rance the sheriff. "Mr. Keenan's mastery of repose, of minute and subtle stage business, amounts to something very like genius," asserted this critic. "He lights a cigar, and the spectator watches the match as he would watch the fuse of a dynamite bomb; he comes out of a blizzard, and, standing motionless in the center of the stage, warms an index finger by boring the tip of it into the palm of his hand, and for some mysterious reason you are thrilled in every fibre."[15]

Such naturalistic details, of which countless examples in the production could be cited, contributed as fully as the sensational effect of the dripping blood to the overall impact and character of the performance. It is, moreover, typical of Belasco's approach to his material, both as a dramatist and as a director, that the drop-of-blood incident was not included for mere shock value but was utilized to stress significant character traits in the Girl and in Jack Rance. Even more than the others in the play, each of whom gambles in his own way for luck, the sheriff is an inveterate gambler. In a final desperate bid to save her lover, Minnie takes advantage of Rance's gambling instinct by challenging him to a poker game, staking herself against Johnson's life. They play, and the Girl, securing her luck at the last instant by exchanging cards, wins. The sheriff stoically departs. The scenic vitality of this episode depended, in turn, on the deliberate physical actions connected with the poker game. Its resounding success in performance is indicated by the fact that Belasco repeated "the business of throwing cards" as a "picture" at the first of the customary curtain calls following the act.

The dependence of *The Girl of the Golden West* upon its intricate weave of stage business became apparent when Belasco attempted to transfer his naturalistic methods to the operatic stage in directing *La Fanciulla del West* at the Metropolitan Opera. The difficulties he encountered proved considerable. "Men and women by the scores and fifties would troop out onto the stage, range themselves in rows, and become merely a background for the principals," the master of stage realism later recorded with dismay. "Then, for no clear purpose, they would all begin to shrug their shoulders, grimace, and gesticulate with their hands." His approach to this problem (which has by no means been eliminated in opera productions of the present day) paralleled his method of staging his own play. "I located the ones who shrugged too much and either backed them up against trees and rocks or invented bits of 'business' by which they were held by the others. When a chorus-singer became incorrigible in the use of his arms I made him go through entire scenes with his hands in his pockets. Little by little I tamed this wriggling crowd."[16]

In a similar way the stars in the opera were compelled to observe a realistic behavior pattern. Belasco made every effort to discourage the customary grand opera convention of stepping to the front of the stage and singing with very little effort to impersonate character. Emmy Destinn was required to sing while she tended bar. Even the immortal

Caruso was asked to deliver his opening phrases as he entered the bar with his back to the audience; later he sang an aria while mounting a steep ladder to the loft of Minnie's cabin. "The result of David Belasco's work was apparent," wrote one of the enthusiastic reviewers of the opera's première, "for a more realistic production has never been seen on the Metropolitan stage. Never has an operatic mob acted with such spirit as did this gang of miners and cowpunchers in the last act; and all through the production there were just those little touches that stamp a Belasco production."[17]

In the third act of his own version of *The Girl of the Golden West*, the customary Belascoan touches again recreated an atmospheric genre picture similar to that of the first act. This act also took place in the Polka Saloon, this time in the dancehall from which a view of the bar used earlier could be glimpsed and recognized by the audience. This factor of recognition, also exploited in the first act, was a shrewd directorial technique to establish audience identification with the scenic environment, thereby heightening the illusion of reality. In contrast to the two previous acts which took place at night, it was now daytime and Belasco's lighting suggested a bright winter morning. The principal feature of this act, which included as many people on stage as the opening scene, was the colorful variation of character grouping and interaction. The climax was reached with the appearance of Dick Johnson, captured by the miners who have decided to take the law in their own hands; again the Girl intervenes and the tenderness of her farewell to her lover persuades the sensitive Sonora and his colleagues to flout Rance's intentions and spare Dick from the gallows. In terms of theatrical value, however, these events added little of fresh interest;

in the opera version of *The Girl of the Golden West,* the relative weakness of the play's third act was compensated for by combining it with the following act, set in the foothills of the Sierras at dawn. It was for this fourth act, actually only a concluding epilogue, that Belasco saved his final stroke of theatricality, summing up in a few short minutes all the rich and vivid picturesqueness for which his production style was justly celebrated.

Belasco's final scene picture in *The Girl of the Golden West* presented "the boundless prairies of the West. On the way East, at the dawn of a day." The decor depicted a great panoramic expanse of prairie. In the far background foothills could be glimpsed, with suggestions here and there of the winding trail leading westward. "The foliage is the pale green of sage brush—the hills the deeper green of pine and hemlock." In the foreground center was a small tepee rudely constructed of two blankets on crossed sticks, obviously only a makeshift shelter for the night. Behind the tent an old tree stump stood out against the horizon. The stage floor was raked with a series of platforms and dotted with little clumps of grass, bushes, small mounds of earth, and rocks. A log fire was seen burning to the left of the tepee.

The curtain rose on a stage in total darkness; "every light on stage and in the house out," warns the promptbook cue. Three gauze curtains hung at the front of the set were slowly raised, one after another; a fourth scrim remained in place throughout the act, enhancing the soft, far-away quality of the picture. As the gauze curtains rose blue footlights and borders, the last traces of night, were brought up to reveal, at first, the glow of a cigarette, then Dick Johnson lying on the grass against a saddle, and finally the Girl entering from the tepee.

Minnie's line, "Look! The dawn is breaking in the East —far away—fair and clear," was the cue for the spectacular climax of the production, the scenic re-creation of a Californian sunrise over the Sierra Nevadas which belongs among the legendary achievements of the wizard of the switchboard. According to Belasco's own account, he experimented without success for three months and expended $5,000 before he was able to capture precisely the right, soft coloring and tone of a distinctly Californian sunrise.[18] Finally, however, he accomplished his aim. The blue of the fading night gradually gave way to the breaking dawn. A glimmer of the first dim rays of the rising sun was seen on the foliage of the foothills. Slowly the light became stronger, illuminating everything in the clear, soft hues of early morning and casting the two figures into bold relief against the horizon. Outcasts from Paradise, on their way to a new life in the East, the lovers turned to look back at the mountains in the brilliance of the sunrise. Minnie, striking the pose shown in the charming photograph reproduced in Figure 11, spoke the final curtain line, Belasco's romantic and deeply personal farewell to the Golden West of memory:

> Oh, my mountains—I'm leaving you———Oh, my California, I'm leaving you———Oh, my lovely West— (*Raising right hand toward R.*)—my Sierras! I'm leaving you! Oh, my—(*Turning to Johnson, going to him and resting in his arms*)—my home.

And once heard, one continues to hear the mournful refrain which Puccini's miners sing in reply:

> *Mai più ritornerai,*
> *Mai più, mai più. . . .*

## CHAPTER SIX

# Sociological Realism: "The Easiest Way"

FROM THE ROMANTIC BRILLIANCE of a California sunrise David Belasco moved into the cold, grey light of didactic naturalism with his production in 1909 of Eugene Walter's *The Easiest Way*, "an American play," according to the program, "concerning a peculiar phase of New York life." A storm of comment was forthcoming. "Mr. Eugene Walter's play . . . is one of the most obnoxious specimens of theatrical trash that have been obtruded on the modern Stage," declared a disgusted William Winter. "It depicts a segment of experience in the life of a shallow, weak, and vain prostitute, who makes a feeble attempt to reform, but who fails to do so. No lover of Dramatic Art, no admirer of David Belasco, can feel anything but regret that he should give the authority of his great managerial reputation . . . and the benefit of his genius and rich professional resources to the exposition of a drama that cannot do good. We do not want to see in the Theatre the vileness that should be shunned; we want to see the beauty that should be emulated and loved."[1]

161

Although considerable shock over the starkly realistic nature of this play reverberated in many reviews of the opening, the production nevertheless became one of Belasco's most resounding successes as well as his major contribution to the performance of sociological realism. Critics were generally impressed as well as taken aback by a production which Charles Darnton of the *New York Evening World* (January 20, 1909) termed "an evening of good acting and bad morals." "*The Easiest Way* is certainly a 'slice of life,'" concluded Alan Dale in the *New York American* (January 20, 1909) reluctantly. But for precisely this very reason other, more progressive critics hailed the drama as "one of the most significant American plays of recent years," praising Belasco for his direction and for the fact that he had allied himself with "an author who possesses ideas and an uncompromising, almost brutal passion for truth."[2] "If the function of the theatre is to hold the mirror up to nature," asserted yet another critic, "the dramatist is within his rights when he exposes rottenness in the social structure. No one can say that *The Easiest Way* is not a faithful reflection of the life it portrays."[3]

It was as a minutely faithful report on a particular segment of life and society that the production of Eugene Walter's play achieved its impact in the theatre. The strength of *The Easiest Way*, which its author called "more or less purely photographic,"[4] did not rest in any expression of revolutionary ideas or a philosophy of life, but stemmed from its attempt to depict a relentlessly real milieu. This milieu was brought to life in Belasco's *mise-en-scène* with a passion for exactitude, a perfection of detail, and a theatrical brilliance that drew unanimous praise from even the fiercest moralists among the critics. "The play was so well done and so forcefully presented that it gripped," ran a typical judgment in the *New York American*. "It was ugly, unpleasant, distressing—anything you like—also more—but it gripped. . . . It is unmoral; it is Broadway; it is a vicious section of vicious life." Others emphasized the major contribution made by Belasco's "extraordinary elaboration of detail" to "the impression of realism and truth which the play makes upon the audience."[5] "All that stage management could do to create and deepen the impression of reality was done," even Winter was compelled to admit—adding that "the result was a deformity magnificently framed to look like nature."[6] Audiences were apparently as shocked—and attracted— by *The Easiest Way* as the reviewers. Belasco's theatre was crowded until the close of the season, and the play ran for 157 consecutive performances.

It is obvious from the promptbook for this production, which corresponds closely to the somewhat more literate and polished version of *The Easiest Way* published by Montrose J. Moses, that the play's action supplied rich opportunities for the exercise of Belasco's naturalistic flair, not only in the depiction of minutely observed details but also in the treatment of successive, contrasting scenic moods.[7]

The curtain rose, without the kind of introductory tableau encountered in the two foregoing productions, on a scene almost romantic in tone. The first act was played against a background of idyllic and rather unreal beauty, on the terrace of a summer country house in the Rockies near Colorado Springs. "The house is one of unusual pretentiousness, and, to a person not conversant with conditions as they exist in this part of Colorado, the idea might be that such magnificence could not obtain in such a locality." Stage left the house rose in the form of a turret built of rough stone of a brownish color, two stories high and projecting a fourth of the way out on stage. In front of the house an elliptical terrace extended to the right of the stage, over part of which a picturesque canopy fashioned from a Navajo blanket was suspended. Around the balustrade of the terrace, which was furnished with chairs and a small table, trailing vines added to the idyllic quality of the scene, as did the backdrop view of "the rolling foothills and lofty peaks of the Rockies, with Pike's Peak in the distance, snow-capped and colossal."

During her stay in this pleasant atmosphere Laura Murdock, a minor actress and mistress of a wealthy broker, Willard Brockton, has for the first time in her life fallen sincerely in love with a young reporter, John Madison, who is himself not lacking in worldly experience. She has resolved to renounce her "easy way" of attaining luxury and return to New York to earn her own living, while Madison remains in an attempt to raise money for their marriage. In an extensive description of the backgrounds and histories of the characters before they appear in the drama, which occupies seven closely printed pages at the beginning of the text, Eugene Walter analyzed his heroine and the moral sensationalism at the core of the play with all the objectivity and clinical detachment demanded by Zola of a true naturalist. "Laura Murdock is a type not uncommon in the theatrical life of New York. . . . [Before we meet her] her career was a succession of brilliant *coups* in gaining the confidence and love, not to say the money, of men of all ages and walks of life. Her fascination was as undeniable as her insincerity of purpose. She had never made an honest effort to be an honest woman."[8]

Belasco himself characterized Walter's heroine as "one of those unfortunate women who wish to live in luxury on nothing a week—a pitifully weak, unmoral, constitutionally mendacious creature who drifts to perdition along the path of least resistance," a comment which suggests his somewhat more conciliatory and sentimental approach to the play.[9] The casting of frail, girlish Frances Starr as Laura also served to secure definite audience sympathy for her at the outset, in spite of theoretical moral condemnation. This quality of amelioration in Belasco's directorial concept, was further bolstered by the airy and romantic pictorial background of the opening act, and by his evocation of constantly shifting moods and tones in the stage picture. Miss Starr scored the greatest success of her career as Laura Murdock. The multitude of effective realistic touches in her performance impressed themselves indelibly on her audiences. "*The Easiest Way* is a play people remember," she told Ward Morehouse years later. "People still tell me about the things I did as Laura—brushing the snow off the milk bottle, sewing a glove, sitting on the trunk at the close of the play." The critics were impressed not only with the power and vivacity of her acting, but also with its restraint. "Miss Starr reveals to us a new type of livery lady; a courtesan with all modern improvements, as it were," Channing Pollock observed. "Our Camilles, our Sapphos and our Zazas have been large women with a strong inclination toward gasps, gurgles, eye-rolling and scene-chewing." In contrast, he stressed, "Miss Starr's

Laura is simple, natural, unaffected, exerting a wonderful appeal and making a strong, if unreasonable requisition upon our sympathies."[10]

A strikingly similar approach to the same basic type of play is, incidentally, seen in Belasco's production of *The Lily*, a static domestic drama adapted from a French play by Pierre Wolff and Gaston Leroux and presented in the same year as *The Easiest Way*. Belasco was at this time interested in the possibilities represented by a more sub-dued acting style, dependent on consciously controlled underplaying of emotion; thus, one character in *The Lily* is shown in the third act "spitting out the words with difficulty, showing that his heart is beating rapidly—he is almost breathless at times."[11] The inertia inherent in static realism was, however, counteracted by Belasco in two basic ways: through the use of pictorial scenic effects to reinforce atmosphere or action—in *The Lily* the first act closed with a characteristic Belasco tableau of night-fall, distant singing, and the drowsy tinkle of sheep bells—and through the skillful variation of mood and tone. A typical directorial note for the third act points out that "the two big scenes that terminate this act must be played in *entirely different* keynote."

At the outset of *The Easiest Way*, when Laura confronted Brockton with her decision to leave him, the casual, deliberately underplayed, matter-of-fact tone of the dialogue was allowed to speak for itself, supported by a bare minimum of realistic stage movement and business. However, in a subsequent scene between Laura and Madison, the lovers' emotional pledge of mutual reform and total honesty with one another was reinforced by the director with sound and visual effects calculated to enhance the situation. The time at the rise of the curtain, indicated by tints of purple and amber in the lighting, was late afternoon. As the act developed, the illumination changed to twilight and then to total darkness. "The shadows cross the Pass, and golden light streams across the lower hills and tops the snow-clad peaks," reads the evocative stage direction in the promptbook. This atmospheric effect was further amplified by the sound of a piano inside the house, playing a Chopin Nocturne. At Laura's line, "I think this is my one great chance. I do love you and I want to do just what you said," a handwritten addition in Belasco's manuscript—"Start change blues"—cues the onset of darkness. The gradual lighting change continued until the end of the act, at which point the two men, each confident of his own evaluation of Laura's character, make a sarcastic bargain to deal honestly with one another as well. Brockton will no longer interfere with Laura, but should she falter he will see to it that Madison is informed of his success, of which he is sordidly and firmly convinced: "The truth is never gentle. Most conditions in life are unpleasant, and, if you want to meet them squarely, you have got to realize the unpleasant point of view." The disillusioned irony of Brockton's statement remains a dark pattern in Eugene Walter's play and constitutes its main theme. By the conclusion of this scene, meanwhile, the stage was in almost total blackness. "All that can be seen is the glow of the two cigars. Piano in the next room is heard." As Madison made his exit, leaving his rival alone on the stage "puffing cigar, the red coal of which is alone visible," the curtain slowly descended.

These picturesque visual effects were used by Belasco to counteract the unbroken, static quality that might result in scenes with very little physical action, but they also provided an emphatic contrast to the stark naturalistic interior that followed, among the most admired settings of Belasco and his designer, Ernest Gros. Six months have elapsed before the beginning of the second act, which shows Laura Murdock living in a cheap theatrical boarding house, "second story back," in midtown New York. She is jobless and running out of money. The stage reproduction of the grim sordidness of the environment in which Laura is caught created initial problems for Belasco. In line with his naturalistic aims, his purpose was to present an exact counterpart of a small bedroom in an authentic theatrical rooming house in New York. His attempt to have a set made in his shop failed to satisfy him. As an alternative, he sought out the shabbiest actual boarding house he could locate in the disreputable "Tenderloin" district of New York City, and, in his own words, "bought the entire interior of one of its most dilapidated rooms— patched furniture, threadbare carpet, tarnished and broken gas fixtures, tumbledown cupboards, dingy doors and window casings, and even the faded paper on the walls." Small wonder that the landlady, as Belasco records, regarded him with some astonishment when he offered to replace these things with new furnishings![12] This, then, was presumably the basis for the setting actually presented on Belasco's stage.

Whatever truth there may be in the tale, however, no doubt remains concerning the startlingly authentic quality of the final stage set. "The detail, the touches, the atmosphere are absolutely perfect," declared Alan Dale in the *New York American.* "It is a triumph of stage management. I have seen garrets, and boarding house rooms, and the squalid resorts of the shabby genteel a thousand times, but never did I see anything so unmistakable as Laura Murdock's 'furnished room' in Act II. Its wall paper, its ceiling, its sordid appurtenances, its 'decorations,' its owner, were indescribably real. This room alone beats any stage setting I have ever looked at." The photograph in Figure 12 depicting Laura's tenement room corresponds in every respect to a regrettably unreproducible blueprint of the groundplan in the original promptbook.

The demands made by both director and author of *The Easiest Way* regarding the illusion of absolute reality emerge from the four closely printed pages in the published version describing every single specification of Laura's room.[18] Many of these details are apparent in the production photo. Dominating the room was an old bed—the Belasco trademark again—which symbolized the pervading decay of the entire interior. Tacked on the head of the bed was a picture of John Madison, under which half a dozen cheap, artificial violets were arranged "in pitiful recognition of the girl's love for her absent sweetheart." A dresser against the upstage wall was similarly suggestive of the devastating ugliness of the environment. It was ornamented with old postcards thrust in between the mirror and its frame, another photograph of Madison, and some well-worn ribbons and veils hung on the side. On the dresser a bottle of obviously cheap perfume "purple in color and nearly empty," a powder box and puff, a rouge box, a hand mirror, a small alcohol curling iron heater, curling tongs, comb and brush, and an assortment of other items were scattered to document grim reality; every single item, in business too tedious to catalogue, was *used* during the act.

Belasco continued the furnishing of this chamber of horrors with relentless determination. In one corner of the room, "with the door to outside closet intervening" as it only would in such an establishment, stood a crumbling washstand half filled with water, with soap, toothbrush and holder, and a number of "cheap" toilet articles in evidence. A soiled towel hung on the corner of the washstand; a pair of stockings hung to dry added another touch of tawdriness. The atmosphere was further enhanced by a small table at the foot of the bed, covered with a dirty and ink-stained table cloth and depressingly decorated with "a cheap pitcher, containing some withered carnations."

The overwhelming sense of accumulated reality extended in every direction. Particularly outstanding was a large, old-fashioned wardrobe in which a few old clothes were hung, "most of them a good deal worn and shabby, showing that the owner—Laura Murdock—has had a rather hard time of it since leaving Colorado." An open drawer in the wardrobe was "filled with a lot of rumpled tissue paper and other rubbish," and beside it an old pair of shoes was casually placed. The impression of chaos was further emphasized by numerous magazines and old books scattered atop the wardrobe beside an unused parasol wrapped in tissue paper. As an example of "vigilant attention to detail" in a production in which he found that "nothing was forgotten," William Winter was particularly impressed with this "rickety wardrobe, with doors that will not close and disordered sheets of music and other truck piled on top of it."[14] This component of the wretched environment was also drawn into the action to provide welcome comic relief. Hence the promptbook indicates that when the maid comes to tidy up the room, she "sees doors of wardrobe have swung open; she crosses, slams them shut." An instant later "doors have swung open again; they hit her in the back. She turns and bangs them with all her strength."

The massive onslaught of crushing detail in this act was as central to the total effect as the dialogue itself. The milieu created by this detail did not provide simply a passive illusion of an authentic boarding house, but also actively expressed and determined the character of Laura, its inhabitant. The lengths to which the production went to paint in measured dimensions the life and situation of the heroine in lifelike terms are apparent from the following typical excerpt:

> Under the mattress at the head of the bed is a heavy cardboard box, about thirty inches long, seven inches wide, and four inches deep, containing about one hundred and twenty-five letters and eighty telegrams, tied in about eight bundles with dainty ribbon. One bundle must contain all practical letters of several closely written pages each, each letter having been opened. They must be written upon business paper and envelopes, such as are used in newspaper offices and by business men.

One of Laura's first actions upon entering the room at the beginning of the act, after having looked "lovingly at the picture of John Madison," is to get out this letter box, open it, select a bundle of letters, untie the ribbon, and extract a letter. "She glances it over, puts it down in her lap, and again takes a long look at the picture of John Madison." These letters definitely do not, however, as one scholar has asserted, "turn out to be the same overworked letters that had served to keep the plots of well-made plays in motion since the days of Eugène Scribe."[15] They have, in fact, no direct function in the plot of the play whatsoever, and their purpose is solely a theatrical one. They were meant to contribute to the unflinching verisimilitude of the stage picture, thereby serving as a vivid illustration of Belasco's naturalistic dictum that truth on the stage led directly to the truth of reality: "I believe in real things on the stage instead of artificial properties, not so much for the audience to see as for actual contact with the actors. . . . If the actors are thoroughly steeped in the atmosphere, they will radiate it, and there comes the real artistry, the thing for which it seems to me producers should be working."[16]

Belasco himself considered his second act setting for *The Easiest Way* one of the most truthful he had ever mounted. At variance with the younger generation in the theatre which had begun to maintain that such things as authenticity and accuracy of detail had no place on the stage, Belasco viewed Walter's play as a typical instance of the fact that "a director has to conform his taste to the material he has in hand. . . . A boarding-house room on the top floor cannot be treated in any other way than as a boarding-house room," he insisted, with full justification in the case of Walter's rigidly naturalistic drama. "I do not say there is no suggestion in realism; it is unwise to clutter the stage with needless detail. But we cannot idealize a little sordid ice-box where a working girl keeps her miserable supper; we cannot symbolize a broken jug standing in a wash-basin of loud design. Those are the necessary evils of a boarding-house, and I must be true to them."[17]

Both Belasco and his author were uncompromising in
their purpose of exposing the evils of this sordid environment, which is presented as an overwhelming deterministic force closing in on the heroine. The play's relentless
quality was due, as Montrose Moses perceived, "not so
predominantly to the moral downgrade of the woman, as
to the moral downgrade of a certain phase of life which
engulfs those nearest the centre of it."[18] Even the theatre
which Laura is attempting to break into is portrayed by
a seedy theatrical agent, in the scene shown in the photograph, as the conventional den of iniquity. About to be
swallowed by her milieu and having been left little
choice by her deterministically minded creator, Laura is
easy prey when temptation appears, in the guise of an old
girl friend, Elfie St. Clair, a tart of gold "gorgeously
gowned in the rather extreme style affected by the usual
New York woman who is cared for by a gentleman of
wealth and who has not gone through the formality of
matrimonial alliance." Laura's backslide was visualized
throughout by Belasco in terms of business. Elfie "leads
Laura over to dresser, takes powder puff and powders
Laura's face ... daubing Laura's face with the rouge paw."
By the act curtain the picture of the "fallen woman" was
complete: "Her hair is half down, hanging loosely over
her shoulders. Her waist is open at the throat, collar off,
and she has the appearance of a woman's untidiness when
she is at that particular stage of her toilet." Incapable of
writing to Madison as Brockton has ordered, she destroys
her note; "slowly Laura puts the letter over the flame of
the alcohol lamp and it ignites. As it burns she holds it
in her fingers, and when half consumed throws it into
waste-jar, sits on side of bed watching letter burn, then

lies down across bed on her elbows, her chin in her hands, facing audience." As the last flicker of the flame died out in this pensive tableau, the second-act curtain fell.

The atmosphere of crumbling decay continued through the last two acts, which take place in "an expensive hotel" two months later. The furnishings were in good taste, not particularly gaudy yet "without the variety of arrangement which would naturally obtain in a room occupied by people a bit more particular concerning their surroundings." Although the reviewer for the *New York American* noted that "the room in the 'expensive hotel' was a gorgeous picture," this setting obviously did not present the same challenge to Belasco's theatrical imagination as the furnished room in the previous act. Its dominant tone and atmosphere were naturalistically established by what an indignant William Winter called "the picturesquely, discretely arranged disorder of the opulent apartments, the signs of a drunken orgy, and the artfully disclosed and disordered bed."[19]

Carelessly discarded evening clothes, a man's cutaway and vest, an opera cloak, gloves, and a silk hat scattered about the room made it obvious from the outset "that the occupants must have returned rather late at night." The impression of the morning after was further stressed by the half-drawn curtains and shades before the windows, "so that when the curtain goes up the place is in rather dim light." Madison, of course, returns from the West, Brockton threatens to reveal Laura's relapse to "the easiest way," and she drives the latter from the hotel room in a stormwind of emotionality. The manuscript promptbook is more explicit than the printed version concerning the climactic tableau with which Belasco ended the act. Laura stood "screaming after him," then crossed the stage to get a dress, recrossed to the trunk, and knelt beside it to pack the dress, ad libbing continuously between sobs: "I want to be happy. I'm going to be married. I'm going to be happy! Get out! Get out! Get out!" She stood "almost screaming these words" as the curtain descended. This was a moment for Belasco's multiple curtains, however, and it rose quickly again to show Laura "as she kneels before trunk putting in dress." A second curtain tableau revealed her "sitting beside trunk, hysterical."

The hectic hysteria and emotionality which dominated the final acts were visually underscored in the fourth act by the pervasive impression of chaos and departure. Two large trunks and a smaller one stood on the stage. All bric-a-brac was gone from the dresser. Drawers stood half open, old pieces of tissue paper and ribbons hung out, torn-up letters, time tables, bottles, and empty boxes littered the room. It "has the general appearance of having been stripped of all personal belongings. There are old magazines and tissue paper all over the place," notes the script.

In a series of tense confrontations between the three main characters, culminating in Laura's frantic threat of suicide, John Madison discovers that Laura has deceived him—and simply walks out on her. "Camille, dying of consumption to slow music in the arms of the forgiving Armand, has at least a sentimental finish that never fails to excite the tear-ducts of the tender matinée maiden," observed one critic in comparing the disillusionment of *The Easiest Way* to the popular Dumas melodrama. "The ending of the Walter play shocks by its frank brutality, and perhaps the moral lesson conveyed is the stronger for it. No one can watch that tense closing scene where Laura Murdock, repudiated and despised by the men she has tricked, sees that the only course left to her is to return

to the old life, without being gripped by the tragedy of it
—the tragedy of a human soul irrevocably damned."[20] The
deterministic naturalism of *The Easiest Way*'s open-ended
technique made a powerful impression on contemporary
viewers. "This story is the story of a life that was of no consequence (so far as a human life is ever of no consequence)," remarked Walter Prichard Eaton, "but a life
that brought woe to others and dull misery to itself. This
life goes on after the final curtain falls, goes on to a conclusion more terrible than the incidents of the play."[21]
The closing lines became proverbial: "Dress up my body
and paint my face. It's all they have left of me," Laura tells
her maid. "I'm going to Rector's to make a hit, and to hell
with the rest!"[22]

Belasco's final stroke of realistic direction was to add an
audiovisual effect emphasizing the grim open-endedness
of the situation. On Laura's final line, "the hurdy-gurdy in
the street, presumably immediately under her window,
begins to the tune of 'Bon-Bon Buddie, My Chocolate
Drop,'" a shatteringly banal melody used in the previous
act as a comment on the vulgarity of the environment.
(The hand-organ man returns, ironically, to grind out the
same tune on Jim Harris's street corner in the second scene
of O'Neill's *All God's Chillun Got Wings*, produced in
1924.) "There is something in this ragtime melody which
is particularly and peculiarly suggestive of the low life, the
criminality and prostitution that constitute the night excitement of that section of New York City," remarks Belasco in one of his methodical notations. "The tune—its
association—is like spreading before Laura's eyes a panorama of the inevitable depravity that awaits her. She is
torn from every ideal that she so weakly endeavored to

grasp." Laura was left standing with a flashy dress in one hand and an equally exaggerated picture hat in the other, "nearly prostrate by the tune and the realization of the future as it is terrifyingly conveyed to her." (In O'Neill's "borrowing" of this moment, the effect of the tawdry melody is similarly to underscore Jim's disillusioned realization that "We're both niggers.") As Laura staggered from the room, her maid, in the process of unpacking the trunk which she had packed with such emotionality in the previous act, mechanically picked up the melody and began to hum it to the accompaniment of the hurdy-gurdy as the curtain slowly descended.

Eugene Walter's play retained its reputation as a significant milestone of the naturalistic theatre in America long after Belasco first presented it; *"The Easiest Way,"* asserted Oliver M. Sayler in 1923, "is the most significant play [Belasco] has ever produced."[23] As was the case with all important Belasco successes, Walter's drama was subsequently revived. "When it began its long and prosperous run at the Belasco Theatre back in January of the winter of 1909 it was the best play in town. It still is that," reported Alexander Woollcott at the re-première in 1921, singling out *The Easiest Way* as "the most creditable achievement, all in all, of David Belasco's long and variegated record as a producer."[24]

Despite its length and its variety, however, Belasco's sixty-year record in the theatre was not yet complete. At least one more very important production, revealing yet another aspect of his theatrical style, was still to follow: his long-awaited revival of Shakespeare's *The Merchant of Venice.*

## CHAPTER SEVEN

# Shakespeare and Naturalism: "The Merchant of Venice"

THE FIRST VISIT to the United States by the Moscow Art Theatre during the season of 1922-1923 provided more than just an opportunity for New York's theatre public to admire performances by one of the world's finest and most acclaimed acting companies.[1] It was also the occasion for comparison of the theatrical achievements of Moscow and Broadway. Following a visit, on February 1, 1923, to David Belasco's production of *The Merchant of Venice* at the Lyceum, Constantin Stanislavski recorded his impressions in a letter to his associate, Vladimir Nemirovitch-Danchenko. These impressions deserve to be recounted rather fully, because they provide us with a valuable key to the significance of the work of the American theatre's master of naturalism as a Shakespearean director. "It is a great mistake to suppose that they don't know good actors here," noted Stanislavski. "The whole theatrical business in America is based on the personality of the actor.... Plus the most lavish production, *such as we don't know*. Plus the most marvellous lighting equipment, about which we have no idea. Plus stage technique which we have never dreamt of. Plus a staff of stagehands and their foremen, we don't even dare to dream of. . . . So we cannot hope to surprise America in every sphere of our art. Such an actor as David Warfield, whom I saw in the part of Shylock, we have not got. And Belasco's production of *The Merchant of Venice* exceeds in sheer lavishness anything I ever saw, and as for its technical achievements the Maly Theatre could envy them. To tell you the truth, I have often wondered why the Americans praise us so much."[2]

Belasco's *Merchant of Venice*, which opened at the Lyceum Theatre on December 21, 1922, to enjoy a run of no less than ninety-two New York performances—an American record for this play—impressed not merely Stanislavski but also the New York critics with its scenic splendor and lavishness. This production, Belasco's solitary adventure in the realm of Shakespearean presentation, proved to be a pinnacle in his long career in the theatre. In its style, moreover, this performance represents a significant culmination in this country of the venerable tradition of producing Shakespeare with pictorial fidelity, in a setting as veritably real and as splendidly authentic as possible. Belasco's production book for *The Merchant of Venice*, together with an elaborate souvenir album of photographs of the performance, were privately printed.[3] Because of their completeness these sources enable us to form a reliable impression of Belasco's artistic intentions as a director in this production, illuminating from yet another angle his specific aims and methods as they found expression in his scenic interpretation of Shakespeare's comedy.

Already during his youthful days on the West Coast, Belasco was exposed to the acting traditions for *The Mer-*

*chant of Venice.* Performing the role of Shylock he saw such great players as John McCullough, Lawrence Barrett, Barry Sullivan, Edwin Booth, and William E. Sheridan. He had, in his own words, assisted in presenting this and other Shakespearean plays "with, be it said, a simplicity of scenic investiture which would cause productions made 'in the Elizabethan manner' to appear as lavishly overcrowded with ornament!"[4] When he set about mounting the play on Broadway, however, he stamped his production with those same qualities that had already established him as the master of elaborate scenic naturalism and theatrical wizardry on the American stage.

As a typical naturalist, Belasco began preparations for producing *The Merchant of Venice* by undertaking a laborious examination of pertinent scholarship and of the play's specific locale. He could quote critic Charles Knight as an authority for the assumption that "the Venice of Shakespeare's own time, and the manners of that city, are delineated with matchless accuracy in this drama,"[5] and that the setting of the play should therefore correspond to the period of its composition. Having found composition dates varying "from 1594 to 1598," Belasco nonetheless decided to depart slightly from them. His reasons for this decision are of interest because they provide a salient clue to the nature of his production. "To me it has long seemed that *The Merchant of Venice* was well described by the late Richard Mansfield as 'a fairy tale,'—that is, as wholly a figment of fancy, fittingly localized in any Venetian period remote enough to be romantic and colorful enough to be picturesque," he argued. "Therefore, without attempting contribution to the fog of scholarly dispute as to when it was written, I have placed the period of its action at about the first quarter of the sixteenth century. That was what may be called The Golden Age of Venice—the time when she had touched the highest point of all her greatness; when, resplendent in the full meridian of her glory, she seemed, indeed, a jeweled queen of the summer seas. Selection of that time, accordingly, permits me to provide for this lovely comedy not only romantic environment but, also, pleasingly novel as well as beautiful costuming."[6]

The fact that romantic and superbly beautiful stage environment and costuming became hallmarks of Belasco's *Merchant* is confirmed by virtually all critics who saw the production. "It is worthwhile," commented Stark Young, "almost as one goes to a museum—going to *The Merchant of Venice* to see the brocades, the incomparable splendor of the textiles that the actors wear, and to see the reminiscences of Titian, Tintoretto, and Veronese in some of the figures of the stage. In themselves—whether they are dramatically wise or not—all these are magnificent."[7] The question of the actual historical accuracy of the Venetian milieu re-created by Belasco may be passed over as being of minor importance in this connection. What matters is the basic attitude toward the comedy's theatrical tone, which he defined as one of pictorial authenticity closely allied with a mood of romantic color and picturesque remoteness.

The stage form in which Belasco chose to interpret *The Merchant of Venice* is thus clearly rooted in the nineteenth-century Shakespearean tradition of Augustin Daly, Irving, and Beerbohm Tree—a connection noted by John Corbin in his *New York Times* review of December 22, 1922. All three of these managers were avowedly admired by Belasco; particularly Henry Irving, he remarks, "was (in my judgment) the greatest stage producer that ever lived."[8] Although David Belasco's production differed, as we shall see, in several significant ways from this nine-teenth-century tradition and bore a stamp which was uniquely his own, he felt strongly about that which to him was a great and time-honored convention of theatrical representation. At a time in the American theatre when new voices were calling for simplification and stylization to replace naturalism and were attracting more attention than ever, Belasco—quite naturally—felt it necessary to take up the question of presenting Shakespeare on an almost bare stage. Such presentation, he found, could appeal only to a small minority of the theatre public interested in mere rhetoric and declamation. Replying as it were to such proponents of the New Stagecraft as Robert Ed-mond Jones, who held that "in the theatre the actual thing is never the exciting thing" and "the designer must always be on his guard against being too explicit,"[9] Belasco asserted: "The immense majority prefers and demands (and is therein reasonable and right) representations designed to create illusions: representations wherein . . . stage direc-tors strive to suit the scenic investiture to the indications of time and place and to the dramatic and histrionic needs of plays presented."[10] It remained a basic principle through-out his career that the main and essential aim of a pro-ducer is to create *"illusion* and *effect."* The supreme goal of all his work was to approximate nature and to present as lifelike a scenic milieu as possible. With this goal clearly in mind he approached Shakespeare.

It is already obvious that Belasco considered naturalism the high point of a century of development and progress

in the theatre. In increasing numbers, however, others—
from William Poël to the champions of the New Stagecraft—saw matters in an entirely different light. Their
idea of attempting to recapture the staging principles, and
thereby the spirit, of Shakespeare's own stage, disregard-
ing in the process "all the expedients, devices, and improvements which incessant study and continuous scientific discovery and invention have developed during the
last three hundred years," appeared completely absurd to
Belasco. "Should he [the director] throw away ambition,
and with it all the advancement that has been made in
that long time, and revert to the crude, inferior, wholly
inadequate methods which were in vogue (and which
were condemned while they were in vogue) during the
infancy of the modern theatre?"[11] Belasco's question is
bitter, dramatic, and wholly rhetorical. He refused to believe that the public would support such an experiment;
nor was there any doubt in his mind that "Shakespeare
himself would eagerly have employed all the many invaluable accessories of modern stagecraft if they had been
available to him. Therefore," he continues, "in making
this revival of *The Merchant of Venice* what I am sure
Shakespeare would have done, what I am sure he would
do if he were here today, that I have done—and availed
myself to the full of those accessories and aids to effect."[12]

Hence Belasco's staging of *Merchant* became a conscious effort—probably the last of its kind in America—
not to disregard the best of the stage traditions with which
earlier outstanding producers had enhanced Shakespeare's
comedy, building on the basis of these "neither as a blind
adherent to old ways nor as a mere presumptuous innovator." In making this effort he expressed his artistic intent

thus: "Only by utilizing *all* that is best . . . in old and tried methods, together with all that is of manifest value in new ones, can a dramatic director give to his public what that public is entitled to receive."[13] For those who might launch the venerable complaint, brought earlier against both Kean and Irving, that scenic accessories and pictorial representation tend to swallow Shakespeare's poetry, Belasco had a ready reply: "A diamond is always a diamond—but cut, polished, and placed in a suitable and lovely setting it always shows to better advantage than when left, rough and imperfect, imbedded in clay."[14]

The setting in which David Belasco actually presented his Shakespearean diamond fully justified his original concept. The *New York Evening World* called his *Merchant* "the greatest production of our greatest producer."[15] In the eyes of John Corbin, critic for the *New York Times*, "opulent good taste could not do more to provide a variety of form and color, ravishing the scenes. . . . Seldom or never has pictorial Shakespeare been more beautiful." The *New York American* observed that "the gorgeousness of the Irving and the Tree productions, the sumptuousness of the old Daly revivals, all sank, belittled, by the side of this. It was neither gaudy nor garish. It was neither too colored nor too massively imposing. Soft tints, exquisite costumes, shaded lighting and the strains of perfect music drifted through the evening." The *New York Tribune*'s eloquent praise of the "rich, hypnotic pictures" in the Belasco production enables us to recapture some of the calculated fascination of its atmosphere of romantic verisimilitude: "[Belasco] gives you Venice, sun-flecked and shadow stricken, and always full of movement and color, with the lines of its stately architecture outlined against an Italian sky. The garden at Belmont is unconceivably [sic] beautiful as an example of its kind, and all the pictures are as perfect as such spurious things can possibly be."

A Shakespearean production of this type, presented in a succession of visually ornate scenic pictures, has traditionally suffered from the difficulty of long waits in the performance while scenery is changed. Moreover, Belasco's naturalistic predilection for massive, three-dimensional scenery—the *New York Evening Telegram* speaks of the "solidness of construction" in the scenery, and the *New York Evening Mail* refers to "massive buildings and deep perspectives"—did nothing to diminish this inherent problem. Despite his assertion that his stage version, in five acts and eleven scenes, several of which were played without pause, was arranged for a "contemporary audience ... that craves fluently continuous movement; that will not assemble in the theatre earlier than eight-fifteen, and that, as a whole, will not remain there later, at the latest, than a few minutes after eleven," elaborate scene changes caused it to last until a quarter past midnight. The text was cut, condensed, and partly rearranged to facilitate the various pictorial effects; in so doing, Belasco depended largely on the stage versions of Irving, Edwin Booth, and Charles Kean. From a practical viewpoint his most important textual changes included grouping a number of the Shylock scenes into the second act and moving the Belmont scenes to the third act. The complete arrangement of scenes as listed in the prompt copy provides eloquent testimony concerning the manner in which Belasco approached the text:

FIRST ACT

First Scene, Venice; A Street, near to the Rialto. Time, Morning.

Second Scene, Belmont; A Room in the House of Portia. Time, Evening.

Third Scene, Venice; An Open Place, before a Synagogue. Time, Late Afternoon.

SECOND ACT

First Scene, Venice; The House of Shylock. Time, Dusk darkening to Night.

Second Scene (without pause), A Room in the House of Shylock.

An indeterminate lapse of time is supposed between the Second and Third Scenes. In presentation there will be the briefest possible interval between them.

Third Scene, The House of Shylock again. Time, Morning.

THIRD ACT

First Scene, Belmont; The Casket Chamber in the House of Portia. Time, Forenoon.

The Tableaux Curtain will be closed for one minute at the end of this scene.

Second Scene, The Casket Chamber again. Time, the next night.

The Tableaux Curtain will be closed for one minute at the end of this scene.

Another interval of a day and the double wedding (of Bassanio and Portia, Gratiano and Nerissa) is here supposed.

## *The Merchant of Venice*

Third Scene, The Casket Chamber again. Time, at Sunset, the next day.

FOURTH ACT

Scene, Venice; A Court of Justice. Time, Midday.

FIFTH ACT

Scene, Belmont; A Garden to the House of Portia. Time, Midnight.

This adaptation of the comedy's text should, meanwhile, not be considered from a literary viewpoint—which is outside the present frame of reference—but against the background of the theatre of naturalism. Seen in this way its chief function was to avoid impossible delay in shifting the three-dimensional scenery. With the exception of the *New York Times* critic, who objected that Belasco's version replaced Shakespeare's color scheme of character and emotion with the color scheme of the designer, Ernest Gros, reviewers generally agreed that the performance achieved a delicate balance of dramatic moods that was carefully integrated with the lavish scenic splendor.

The theatrical tradition of performing *The Merchant of Venice* in a manner which presents not merely Shakespeare's comedy but also a wide, bustling picture of Venetian life has, of course, its roots in the nineteenth century. Charles Kean's celebrated *Merchant* production brought to the stage the bridges, the canals, the gondolas, the crowds, and the carnival mummers of Venice in a dazzling exhibition.[16] Later, Henry Irving and others carried forward this tradition of an "authentic" Venice laden with real details—Piazza San Marco, the Rialto, real palaces,

187

practicable bridges built over real canals, floating gondolas—and thronged the stage with lively crowds of masked
Venetian carnival-goers arriving in the gondolas, dashing
across the bridges, and forming colorful *tableaux vivants*.[17] Belasco, however, departed in a significant manner from this stage tradition. Despite his avowed admiration for Irving and although illusionistic scenic investiture
was still a primary and vital concern for him, he made use
of opulent pageantry in aspects of staging rather than in
the setting itself. The Venice which he and his designer,
Ernest Gros, created was, as we have already heard, a
Venice "remote enough to be romantic and colorful
enough to be picturesque." Hence he dispensed entirely
with the traditional archeological verisimilitude of Piazza
San Marco, the view of the Rialto, and the Venetian canals with their familiar bridges. Such historical realism,
brought into disrepute by the advocates of the New Stagecraft, had lost its fascination for a 1922 audience.

Looking at the photographs of the pictorially striking
sets for Belasco's *Merchant* today, one tends to agree with
Stark Young's observation: "As for the accuracy of the
Venetian atmosphere afforded . . . one may point out that
these scenes have no particularly inspired Venetian quality
at all; those streets for anything they might achieve might
as well be in the older quarter of Padua, in Vicenza, or
even in an Umbrian hill town like Cortona."[18] Burns
Mantle, writing in the *New York Daily News*, pursued
the point still further, finding, despite Belasco's protests
against modernistic concepts of staging, nonnaturalistic
qualities in the setting that "bridged in a measure the old
and new school of scenic investiture." That which most
obviously contributed to this impression was Belasco's use

of drapes to frame the set, a technique which lent the performance a quality of genuine theatricality. In general, Belasco's choice of setting was clearly consistent with his whole philosophy and practice as a man of the theatre. Throughout his career he insisted upon the use of individualized, realistic details, not for their own sake but as subordinate elements in a carefully integrated, harmonious entity. In such an entity, externals like gondolas, familiar landmarks, and so on—however attractive in themselves— had no particular justification or function.

The stage life with which David Belasco invested *The Merchant of Venice* was one in which a large number of specific details were merged to create a vivid, concrete atmosphere. The opening scene, representing "a street near to the Rialto," was constructed of straight and angular set-pieces as houses, some with practicable doors. The houses extended diagonally across the stage to form a street, running from center to stage right and backed by a street drop at the rear. Behind another house set-piece stage left, just above the tormentor, another smaller street ran off to the left. The lighting indicated the time of day as morning. As the curtains parted, a boy carrying a basket of cherries was discovered stage center at the foot of the larger street. "He stands in the shadows of the high house and gazes upward, looking from window to window for possible buyers of his fruit," notes the promptbook. Slowly the scene came to life. A man carrying faggots entered down the large street, came downstage, passed the boy without noticing him, and made his exit out the smaller street stage left. A second man, carrying a painting, then entered the larger street, this time through a house door. He came downstage, stopped, and spoke to the boy, apparently in pantomime, "as though telling him of a buyer within the house." He then continued on, exiting through the smaller street. The boy ran to the door of the house indicated, knocked, was admitted, and disappeared. As this took place, a man carrying a wineskin entered from the left; simultaneously Solanio, Antonio, and Salarino entered down the larger street. Meeting them as he turned the corner to pass up the street, the man with the wineskin stepped aside, bowed deferentially, and continued out. Meanwhile, the trio reached the front of the stage and Shakespeare's dialogue was ready to begin.

The three actors were grouped in a conventional semicircle at the footlights, Solanio left, Antonio center and slightly upstage, Salarino right. The positioning of actors in a semicircle at the front of the stage, with the most important character occupying the central position, was a venerable convention that survived long after its original motivation—the dim candle lighting and poor acoustics of the wing-and-border system—had disappeared. It is thus interesting and a little surprising to observe, here as elsewhere, the repeated use of this convention by a naturalist like Belasco, although the shifting and changing positions in his *mise-en-scène* eliminated any trace of formality or stiffness in the stage groupings. In general, the various characters populating this opening scene were not introduced simply to create gratuitous theatrical effect. They were utilized, as were Stanislavski's highly individualized mass scenes in his *Othello*, to achieve a concrete stage atmosphere, thereby throwing the main action into vivid relief.[19] Moreover, through their use of the various components of the setting they established the physical environment as a functioning part of the total theatrical milieu.

In the second scene of the play, "a room in the house of Portia," this milieu assumed a decidedly more abstract character, due no doubt to the elaborate scene change being prepared for the subsequent scene. Thus, Belasco's stage directions for this "carpenter" scene call for drapes and a backdrop with three arches hung downstage at the second wing position. Performance photographs indicate, however, that an even simpler solution was adopted in actual practice: the walls of Portia's room were merely suggested by an effective, semicircular arrangement of drapes on the forestage. The particular character of her room was conveyed by selected pieces of furniture and by an elegant, oriental runner placed diagonally across the floor. Portia was discovered seated on a settee, engaged in needlework. In a similar fashion Ellen Terry had lounged on a sofa during the discussion of her suitors, as had Modjeska.[20]

The third scene of the production was characterized by a series of those lighting effects for which Belasco was widely and justly renowned, and which, more than any other single production aspect, contributed to the heightening of mood and atmosphere in a scene. Depicting an open place before a synagogue and occupying full stage, the third scene began in the light of late afternoon. This gradually faded into a fiery sunset, and then almost to darkness. At the end, as Bassanio and Antonio were leaving the stage, the lights continued "darkening into shadows." As Shylock, "turning slowly" and following them with his gaze, delivered the interpolated lines with which the scene ended in this version,

> Thou call'dst me dog before thou hadst a cause;
> But, since I am a dog, beware my fangs!

the light fell upon him in a dramatically "dull, ruddy glow." An important part of the strength in Belasco's theatrical talent rested in precisely such boldly underscored effects as this. He was personally convinced that "the complete play is impressive and fulfils its purpose only to the extent that it carries an audience back to its own experiences. If my productions," he argued, "have an appealing quality, it is because I have kept this important fact constantly in mind and have tried, while concealing the mechanism of my scenes, to tug at the hearts of my audience."[21] Whereas other directors in this period—as, for instance, Stanislavski in his *Othello*—frequently permitted realistic effects and a vast pattern of superimposed "business" to lead to a de-emphasis of scenic emotion, the contrary was true of Belasco, whose preference for strongly accentuated and heightened emotionality recalled the earlier ideals of the romantic period.

Not only the lighting but also the entire synagogue set used by Belasco in this scene served to focus and relate the scenic action to Shylock, intensifying the potential drama around his figure. As the curtain rose, the evening service in the synagogue was in progress. The chanting of the cantor and the congregation, and occasionally the voice of the rabbi, were heard. Several belated worshipers arrived, separately, from the right and left entrances, and were admitted through the main door of the synagogue, each one quickly performing the ceremony of hand-washing before going inside. The carefully orchestrated background of sound and physical action created by Belasco was not, however, designed merely to establish an effective scenic "mood" in the generalized sense. For practitioners of naturalism like Belasco or Stanislavski, there was no such thing as generalized atmosphere. In the present case, it is typical of Belasco's technique that he utilized the synagogue scene to introduce a number of characters appearing later in the play, whose presence and behavior added a "natural" aura to the proceedings and provided a realistic motivation—not, of course, present in Shakespeare's play—for Shylock's entrance at this specific time and in this specific place.

The first of the play's characters introduced by Belasco in the synagogue scene was Launcelot Gobbo, discovered standing beside the synagogue door. Jessica then entered through the door; "she goes to Launcelot; they whisper." They leave together, but after a moment Jessica returns alone, re-entering the synagogue. The next to appear were Bassanio and Solanio: "they come to about center, and pause a moment irresolutely, Bassanio being perplexed to know whether or no Shylock is inside the Synagogue." Two Jews, Tubal and Chus, a super introduced by Belasco, then entered downstage left. "Bassanio stops them and questions Tubal, who shakes his head in negation. Tubal and Chus then proceed toward Synagogue door. Tubal, looking off to R.U.E. . . . , sees Shylock approaching. He points him out to Bassanio: then Exeunt Tubal and Chus into Synagogue. Bassanio and Solanio get down R., and exit Solanio, at a gesture by Bassanio, R.F.E. Enter Shylock R.U.E.; as he gets to Synagogue door Bassanio calls him: 'Shylock.' Bassanio goes up to Shylock: they stand in converse near Synagogue door while several other Jews pass in;—then they come forward, Shylock speaking as they do so." The effectiveness of all this elaborate pantomimic byplay was enhanced by the fact that the audience was ignorant of what it was actually about. Nor was the element of suspense thus generated intended as something extraneous from Belasco's hand; it was an integral part of the directorial concept, providing an acceptably "natural" preparation for the appearance of the main characters in the scene.

As a director Belasco sought to prepare for and to integrate everything taking place on his stage, and this technique, as we have seen in the foregoing, was applied with equal vigor in his Shakespearean production. Characteristically, therefore, the second act of his *Merchant* did not open with Launcelot Gobbo's celebrated running-away monologue. Instead, this was slowly prepared for by first letting the scene, depicting the house of Shylock (Fig. 13), take on a life of its own. Shylock's house, its entrance placed downstage left, was located at the confluence of two narrow and sombre streets. When the curtain rose, Tubal entered from the back and crossed down to the entrance of the house. At that moment Chus emerged from the house, "his manner . . . depressed—as though he had just failed in some business negotiation." They exchanged greetings in pantomime, and each then made his exit, Tubal disappearing into Shylock's house. In the doorway Tubal encountered Launcelot Gobbo, who stood respectfully aside for him. When Tubal had passed inside, Launcelot closed the door and moved to the center of the stage. Only then was he ready to begin his monologue.

Belasco's technique of blending light, sound, and movement in order to place the play's dramatic content in high relief culminated in the episodes centering around Jessica's elopement and Shylock's discovery of it. As an atmospheric prelude, during Shylock's exchange with Jessica the stage remained in shadow, deriving most of its illumination from a shaft of orange yellow light streaming from the open door of Shylock's house out onto the stage. Jessica's subsequent elopement with her lover ends, as we know, very quietly in Shakespeare. There is to be no masque after all. But in Belasco's day, quiet endings had long been out of fashion. Hence, in Henry Irving's renowned Lyceum production, after Jessica had fled in a gondola there was a rushing in of revelers, and the curtain fell on a stage flooded with lights, noises, and movement.[22] In Belasco's version these effects began even earlier. Following Shylock's exit and Jessica's line,

> Farewell! and if my fortune be not crost,
> I have a father, you a daughter, lost!

she disappeared from the window from which she spoke this speech. "Music swells. Masquers throng across the stage," notes the promptbook. As the elopement took place and Lorenzo and Jessica were about to make their escape, more masquers came "running on, romping and singing." As the lovers ran off, masquers flooded the stage and then disappeared. Following an effective pause, Shylock appeared at the head of the street. Slowly he came downstage to the door of his house, paused, then raised his hand to grasp the knocker—"as the lights faded."

This interpolation, which originated with Henry Irving and constituted one of his most celebrated moments,[23] is undeniably striking in the theatre, regardless of what one may think of its propriety. As A. C. Sprague has pointed out, the idea of a father's coming home and finding his daughter gone may conceivably have been suggested by the same situation in Verdi's *Rigoletto*; more probably it derived from Victor Hugo's *Le Roi s'amuse*, a favorite acting vehicle in the nineteenth century and the basis for Verdi's opera. "Even so," writes Sprague of Irving, "the business was strikingly original. Its reticence, and the appeal it makes to the imagination are not to be denied."[24] After Irving, this effect was copied in almost every representation of *The Merchant of Venice*.[25] It is no great surprise to find, however, that it remained for David Belasco to add yet another dramatic *coup* to the emotional impact of the charged situation. Thus, following the blackout which punctuated Shylock's arrival at the house, he introduced an entirely new scene and setting: an "austerely simple room" *within* Shylock's house, seen in Figure 14. As the curtain rose, Shylock was heard knocking on the door—seen from the outside in the previous scene but now shown from the inside—and calling: "Why, Jessica, I say!" The knock was repeated; then in an interesting foreshadowing of later cinematic technique, the door swung open and Shylock was revealed standing in the doorway, "amazed at finding his dwelling unguarded." He entered, calling again for his daughter. The sounds of revelry outside, heard faintly, increased. Shylock again went outside still calling for Jessica, re-entered—and stumbled first on a set of keys dropped in the doorway by his daughter and then on a jeweled ring. Snatching these things up and crying, "Jessica, my girl, Jessica!" he saw that a large, iron strongbox had been left open. He uttered "a piercing cry" as he realized that he had been robbed. Turning, he discovered a letter and veil left by Jessica on a table. As he read, the masquers could be heard thronging past outside his house. His passionate outburst, which begins:

Fled with a Christian!—O, my Christian ducats!—
Justice! the law! my ducats, and my daughter!

belongs in fact to Solanio, who in Shakespeare reports on Shylock's reaction (ii, viii). In Belasco's interpretation, however, it too was pressed into service to intensify the effect of the dramatic pathos surrounding the figure of Shylock.

This same emotional tone was continued by the director in the subsequent scene, which contained Shylock's famous Jew-Christian speech (". . . I am a Jew. Hath not a Jew eyes?") and was also played inside the house. Belasco's stage direction regarding Shylock's outward appearance clearly suggests the strong inner turmoil he was aiming for. When Shylock enters "he is without hat, his clothes disordered, his hair disheveled; his face ghastly pale, his eyes blazing, his manner unrestrained and wild. He comes on with a half-running rush." Later, at his lament,

. . . . two thousand ducats gone . . . and no satisfaction, no revenge . . . no sighs but o' my breathing; no tears but o' my shedding,

"Shylock clutches his body garment, tearing it open at the throat and breast, with left hand and beats his breast with right, clenched." The ground was now established for the climactic drama of the trial scene.

Before turning to the treatment of Shylock in this central scene, however, a word must be said about the Belmont scenes and the contrastingly light, romantic tone they contributed to the performance. It will be remembered that Belasco grouped the casket scenes together in the third act of his version of *The Merchant of Venice*. Dominating Ernest Gros's lavish design for the casket chamber was a triple-arch set-piece, stretching across the rear of the scene and joined by corresponding, diagonal side pieces. The entire setting, praised by the *New York Times* as "richly beautiful in the internal decorations" and "looking out on a landscape of vibrant aerial spaces," was backed by a cyclorama affording a view of the Italian countryside (Fig. 15). From this background Portia's suitors entered—first, with a flourish of Moorish trumpets, the Prince of Morocco attended by Moorish soldiers and slaves bearing gifts, then, in the following scene, Bassanio. The Prince of Arragon episode was cut by Belasco, as it had been by Henry Irving.[26] The Belmont scene in the final act, "a garden to the house of Portia"—John Corbin of the *Times* called it "an enchantment of moonlight and stars"—was likewise backed in its entirety by a cyclorama, representing "the night sky studded with stars." The romantic atmosphere of this formal garden, with its wide marble stairway, marble seats, square marble pillars, elevated marble sundial stage center, and a frame of box-hedges, was further enhanced by a musical accompaniment by a Jester playing on a lute and singing "It was a lover and his lass." With this song Belasco opened the act, and with it he ended the play.

In general, meanwhile, the Belmont scenes seem to have held less interest for Belasco as a director. One reason might be the fact that these scenes afforded him less opportunity for realistic byplay and integrated lifelike effects. Apart from adding a variety of affectionate gestures between the lovers, there was comparatively little Belasco could interject in the way of naturalistic detail. Furthermore, the central, dramatic interest in the play was by tradition considered to rest in Shylock's character and actions. In this connection it is worth remembering that, until Henry Irving restored the text, the prevailing theatrical custom had been to conclude the play at the close of the trial scene, ending it with Shylock's departure in Act IV, i.[27] While it would have been inconceivable for Belasco to tailor his version to the prominence of Shylock alone, this character nonetheless remained the most important focal point in the directorial image of this production.

The outward trappings of Belasco's trial scene were impressive—"a riot of rich color and sober ornament, truly Venetian."[28] In a courtroom partly enclosed in blue side drapes but intended to suggest a realistically reproduced chamber in the Palace of the Doges, the principal visual element was the large and colorfully costumed crowd of magnificoes, council members, soldiers, citizens, and others framing the dominant figure of Shylock. Belasco himself described Shylock as "an embodiment . . . of vindictive hatred over-reaching and destroying itself in a hideous purpose of revenge. And he is not the less so because, in his final discomfiture and utter ruin, he is, in some sort, pathetic."[29] Critics such as John Corbin found this note of pathos a predominant characteristic of David Warfield's Shylock. "One feels an ancient bitterness, the bitterness of racial as well as personal persecution that heightens in Shylock's contact with spendthrift and abusive Gentiles to an intense hatred," wrote Corbin, emphasizing that in the trial scene "pathos was there to the last degree."

Belasco brought Shylock into the scene "deliberately and firmly," stopping and then looking around the room for his victim, Antonio. Having located him in the crowd, he "fixes a glare upon him for a moment, then his face becomes mask-like." When Bassanio made him the offer, "For thy three thousand ducats here is six," Shylock advanced slowly to him, "gazing into his eyes: pointing

downward, with a stab-like gesture, at the money-bags."
Then, by kicking one of the bags aside, he indicated
their contemptible lack of power to affect his resolve for
revenge.

Warfield's Shylock "deliberately and carefully" sharp-
ened his knife on the sole of his shoe, going down on one
knee to do so. A little later, he rose and tested the edge
and point of the knife with his thumb. His general attitude throughout the proceedings was one of contemptu-
ous but vigilant attention. Assessing his right—"So says
the bond"—to carve out a pound of Antonio's flesh "nearest his heart," this Shylock indicated, as Irving's had
done,[30] the words in the bond with the point of his knife.

At the climax of the scene, with Portia's speech,

And you must cut this flesh from off his breast:
The law allows it, and the court awards it,

everything became movement. Shylock whirled around to
confront Antonio, who tore open his shirt. Bassanio, about
to throw himself between them, was restrained by Gratiano. A priest advanced. Spectators moved, rising, some
turning away. The Duke himself rose in his seat, as did
several magnificoes and council members. As Shylock
rushed on Antonio, his knife half raised, Portia was compelled to speak her challenge quickly. On "Take then
thy bond," Shylock made "a slight, convulsive movement"
as though about to complete his rush on Antonio, only to
be stopped by Portia's repetition of the phrase and her
ominous warning about the drop of blood. Following
Shylock's defeat, the scene moved swiftly to a conclusion.
Starting to leave the courtroom, Shylock was stopped by
Portia's second challenge: "The law hath yet another

hold on you." Told that he "must be hang'd at the state's charge," he suddenly and dramatically collapsed on the floor before the Duke—the moment captured in the photograph seen in Figure 16.

Defeated and at last escaping from his tormentors, Shylock's final exit re-emphasized Belasco's conception of the character's relentlessness and vindictive hatred coupled with dignity and pathos. In line with earlier stage tradition, Gratiano brutally took hold of Shylock's gown, which the Jew indignantly plucked from his grasp. Staggering and nearly falling, he caught hold of Antonio, but recognizing his adversary he regained his dignity, rallied his strength, and moved on. A monk raised his crucifix, and for an instant Shylock paused. The sound of jeering and hooting broke out. The Jew of Venice was gone.

Stark Young has provided a lucid description that captures the essence of the orientation and effect of Shylock in this climactic scene, "that little, bent, heart-breaking figure of the Jew, with his pious, suffering eyes, fawning, relentless, sharpening his knife, in the midst of that glittering court." "I watched Mr. Warfield and was moved deeply," continues the critic, "as I have been sometimes when I saw some old, ragged father on the East Side who stood on the corner peddling to the people he despised in his heart trifles that he scorned and who had in his eyes so much goodness, unapproachable fanaticism, patience, tragic silence, and distress."[31]

Producing only a single of Shakespeare's plays, Belasco evolved no specific "style" of Shakespearean performance. Although he expressed interest in presenting other Shakespearean plays—at various points he apparently considered performing *Henry IV*, presumably Part 1, and *Julius Cae-*

*sar,* which he regarded as "the greatest play in the world"[32] —this interest had no further practical consequences. Clearly, in his overall approach to *The Merchant of Venice,* as in his particular conception of Shylock, Belasco applied the familiar naturalistic methods and aims of his earlier productions. His powerful directorial personality was never far beneath the surface; "scratch the Shakespeare here and you will find Belasco," wrote Stark Young, "and that is the best thing about the occasion." Like Stanislavski, who in 1927 made him an honorary member of the Moscow Art Theatre, Belasco relied, in this production as always in his scenic art, on a rich weave of recognizable, naturalistic detail and motivation in which to catch his audience, and with which to bring theatrical "truth" to Shakespeare's poetry.

# New Theatres for Old

"THE THEATRE always reflects the taste and proclivities of its own time," Belasco had realized, and during the 1920s, as the winds of artistic change whistled through the flats of the American theatre, Belasco's time seemed to have passed. Not that this final decade of the aging director's sixty-year career in the theatre was devoid of arresting productions. *The Merchant of Venice* had been preceded two years earlier by his presentation of the Granville-Barker version of Sacha Guitry's *Deburau*, hailed as one of the most impressive and beautifully staged productions in the annals of the New York stage; it was followed by such productions as the Belasco version of Guitry's *The Comedian* (1923), *Laugh, Clown, Laugh* (1923), his adaptation of the Pagliacci story starring Lionel Barrymore, and *Mima* (1928), his version of Molnar's *The Red Mill* in which the tireless seventy-five-year-old director's constructivist vision of Hell stunned Broadway audiences, and his modernist technique of sending devils leaping into the auditorium "embarrassed" younger and more conservative critics like St. John Ervine.[1] For all this, however, the implacable new generation of antinaturalistic directors, designers, and playwrights which emerged in the twenties was determined, as we have seen, to regard Belasco as the detested embodiment of the outmoded naturalistic fallacy. Nothing would persuade the newcomers to consider his contributions in their proper context, or to recognize the impact which his harmoniously balanced ensemble work, his revolutionary advances in interpretative lighting, and his unique talent for the creation in his productions of a pervasive mood had on the theatre that came after him. Later scholars, going no further than to the programmatic critics of the twenties for their information, have too often been content to repeat, sometimes word for word, the shopworn phrases of the anti-Belasco stereotype.[2] Yet Montrose Moses was able in 1925 to offer a sensibly balanced view of the situation: "What he wants is not what the younger generation is seeking. And there the gap between them widens. With no real cause, however. . . . There may be groups who hold in their hands equally as virile a contribution to be made. They are opening vistas which Belasco cannot see. But he has already opened vistas which they are not generous enough to recognize. . . . He was in advance of the new movement, and prepared some of the way for it."[3]

As his career drew to a close, Belasco never lost his sensitivity to changing styles and developments in the theatre. Eugene O'Neill had ushered in the excitement of the twenties, and it should perhaps be no surprise that Belasco, who seems to have approached O'Neill earlier, agreed in 1925 to stage an early, sprawling version of the picturesquely exotic *Marco Millions*. An unpublished letter from

Belasco, offering an interesting insight into his attitude toward the young dramatist and his designer, seems to have escaped general notice. It is dated March 19, 1925:

Dear Eugene O'Neill,

The "Mark o' Millions" [sic!] is going to be a real treat to me.

I am delighted and pleased to do it for I think it the very best thing you ever wrote.

I shall try to make it a shining mark in my own life as well.

I am happy to tell you that I have met Robert Edmond Jones. He is to do the scenes for you. I know that this news will please you. We are both going to give you our best.

I have asked Mr. Jones to go to you and he will see you in about 2 or 3 weeks and remain with you a while. You can go over everything with him; then he will come back to me with all he has worked out with you. I want to come with him but I cannot. . . .

May I make a suggestion? Could we not restore the young Princess at the age of eight—nine—or ten years? At one time you had her in, but she was too young. A glimpse of her as you had her before she is the grown-up Princess would be, I think, good. . . .

> Faithfully,
> David Belasco[4]

Although the letter undermines the accepted notion of Belasco's unwillingness to come to terms with the new generation, the production in question was not to be. Belasco dropped his option on the play the following year.

The second powerful vector in the artistic climate of the late twenties was, of course, the exploding technology of the motion picture. "Shadows speak and people are amazed," said Belasco of the medium. "Soon their amazement will give way to an acknowledgment of their limitations." The standard critical assertion that Belasco's style of theatre was better suited to the celluloid of the Hollywood epic ignores—willfully, it almost seems—his own views as well as the fundamental basis of his scenic art. His few expressed opinions about silent films, quite opposed to the more spectacular aspects of a D. W. Griffith, reflect an awareness of the cinema as an art form distinct from theatre. A film should show, he argued, "the mental processes of the characters which so seldom now are even suggested in motion picture plays." Although he entertained no ambition to direct a movie himself, he advocated an approach based on "a very human story adjusted to the simplest backgrounds, with very few characters and no ensemble whatsoever. In inventing the 'business' of the scenes I would contrive to have the hero or heroine hold the stage alone whenever possible, for I would aim to tell the story, not by a correlation of incidents, but by the facial expressions of the actors." "All motion pictures," he maintained, "will come into a closer relation with art when they choose more intimate themes, devote more attention to the detailed development of their stories, and place less reliance upon stars."[5] As interesting as the implications of his views on film may be, however, Belasco's vision remained, from first to last, a theatrical vision, inseparable from the intense immediacy of the living theatre.

Belasco's style of theatre was, as the foregoing chapters have shown, far from inflexible; his naturalism underwent marked changes as his stage became less cluttered and the temper of his scenic art became less tempestuous and more subdued. Nonetheless, until the very end of his career his view of the theatre remained unalterably focused upon the basic naturalistic aesthetic: the belief in the deterministic power of a detailed and emotionally charged stage environment. "Because I believe the theatre is both an art and an applied science," he wrote in 1930, "I apply the rules of science to my productions. Nothing is left to chance. . . . I count time and effort as nothing as against perfection of detail." For Belasco, as for Craig and Reinhardt, the theatre was "a composite of *all* the arts; literature, music, the dance, painting, sculpture—even architecture, for it is three-dimensional."[6] "His mind grasped all phases of a production, just as his vision saw the whole," remembered Walter Prichard Eaton, and hence "he was able to realize, as few ever have, the ideal of the theatre— a single intelligence which can create or at least definitely control text, scenery, and lights, can train and direct the players, and can therefore achieve a complete and unique unity."[7]

As an old man in the midst of a world that had changed radically, we find his own working methods unchanged in a last unpolished workbook from 1931, the final year of his life, containing copious notes for a projected production of an anonymous script called *Virgin City*.[8] "The story of Virginia City is, in reality, a page torn from the early history of the fabulous Nevada town 'before the fire' which wiped out its early pride and glory," noted Belasco, and his watchful demands for accuracy and control speak for themselves. "Let it be understood that the action takes place within two days and that it is winter and cold" is the terse but pregnant warning to the stage manager. A stage direction stating that "E.B., attracted by a sound (unheard) opens the door a little" receives the stern reminder: "If you hear *anything*, you hear *everything*, or it's wrong. You *can't* hear from outside, unless the door is open or *the window broken.*" The classic command from this promptbook, "Get time for dawn in winter in Nevada," has already been singled out earlier. Suggesting that a first-act love scene be moved to a subsequent act ("No man grabs at a girl who has jilted him and left him to sweat it out in prison. It isn't natural!"), Belasco added that "the old theatrical curtain won't do. It's hardboiled and insincere and ridiculous." Intent as always upon avoiding the melodramatic, his alteration of the ending, in which the heroine shoots her betrayer Sam Fanshaw, is instructive. Moving the event itself offstage, he remarked that "I even think it would be effective if she shut the door behind her and we didn't hear the shots, leaving it open on her return. It is evident that Sam has fallen near enough to the door that, when the door is opened, they can all see him; but the audience must not see him." "Never actually reveal on the stage what can be suggested," he had insisted throughout his career.[9]

Even these few promptbook comments are enough to re-emphasize the nature, as well as the limitations, of Belasco's theatrical art. Its obvious Achilles heel, given the wisdom of our critical hindsight, was the less than distinguished repertory upon which its power was sometimes lavished. Its great strength was its magic—that is, intensified and sharply focused—realism and its vigorous totality. Belasco intended his art to be no spiritless copy

208

of reality, but a reinvention of reality that started with reality itself in order to be able to transpose and amplify it in telling his story. His theatre was one of fundamental consistency, firmly bound by a single style and thus acquiring its own truth, its own peculiar meaning and poignancy. Herein lies the source of its great success in its own time as well as the seeds, once the tastes and ideals of that time had altered, of its subsequent decline.

The taste and proclivities of the twenties in America were, as Harold Clurman insists, reflected in an organization like the Theatre Guild, bearing "a collegiate stamp on them" that set them quite apart from "the hearty roughnecks" of the era of David Belasco. "They understood that the cynicism and melancholy of the Continent was [sic] riper and richer than the still green American drama. They were admirers rather than makers. They were imitators rather than initiators." Times soon changed again, however, and the Group Theatre, formed in the year of Belasco's death, became in its turn the "reflection, image, agent, influence, and product" of its own unquiet day.[10] The epoch of Belasco's intense emotionality seemed far behind; little thought was wasted on the significance of his pioneering contributions to American theatre. "The drama went beyond him," wrote Prichard Eaton in 1936:

It has gone, indeed, to a point where emotional excitement and suspense—the life-blood of drama—have often vanished in intellectual debate. I have fancied sometimes as a group of actors talked their way on and on and my mind wandered, that dimly, like Peter Grimm, the shade of a soft-voiced, soft-handed man in a clerical collar, with a heavy lock of gray hair falling across his forehead filtered in from the wings and tried, again like Peter, to "get across." Nobody saw him. Nobody heard him. But I could read his lips.

"My dears, my dears," he was trying to say, "right here a situation, please! Let us go back and try it again."[11]

# Notes

## INTRODUCTION

1 Stark Young, *Immortal Shadows* (New York, 1948), p. 44.
2 In Montrose J. Moses and John Mason Brown, eds., *The American Theatre as Seen by Its Critics* (New York, 1934), p. 230.
3 Walter Prichard Eaton, "Madame Butterfly's Cocoon: A Sketch of David Belasco," *The American Scholar* v (Spring 1936), 182.

## CHAPTER ONE

1 Preface to *Thérèse Raquin*, in Barrett H. Clark, *European Theories of the Drama*, rev. ed. (New York, 1965), pp. 377-378.
2 *Ibid.*, p. 378. See also E. Zola, *Le Naturalisme au théâtre* (Paris, 1881), pp. 89-94, and Gösta M. Bergman, *Den Moderna Teaterns Genombrott 1890-1925* (Stockholm, 1966), pp. 13-17.
3 "Behind the Fourth Wall" in *Directors on Directing*, eds. Toby Cole and H. K. Chinoy (Indianapolis, 1963), p. 94.
4 John Gassner, *Directions in Modern Theatre and Drama* (New York, 1966), p. 21.
5 David Belasco, *The Theatre through Its Stage Door*, ed. Louis V. Defoe (New York, 1919), pp. 202, 231.

6 Cf. the discussion in Mordecai Gorelik, *New Theatres for Old* (New York, 1940), pp. 124-128.

7 "To Begin" in *The Theory of the Modern Stage*, ed. Eric Bentley (Penguin Books, 1968), p. 375.

8 Constantin Stanislavski, *My Life in Art* (New York, 1956), p. 330.

9 On the development of this tradition, see Frederick J. Marker, *Hans Christian Andersen and the Romantic Theatre* (Toronto and Oxford, 1971), esp. pp. 166-206. See also Jytte Wiingaard, *William Bloch og Holberg* (Copenhagen, 1966).

10 William Winter, *The Life of David Belasco* (New York, 1918), I, p. 10.

11 *Jim Black*, a study of deep-dyed villainy in eight acts and fourteen scenes, was laid in the "desperate" city of St. Louis: David Belasco, "My Life's Story," *Hearst's Magazine* xxv (1914), 650. For a list of Belasco's early plays, see *Plays Produced under the Stage Direction of David Belasco* (New York, 1925).

12 Winter, I, p. 40.

13 *Ibid.*, I, p. 14.

14 Interview with David Belasco, *New York Times*, January 31, 1904.

15 Cf. *Plays Produced under the Stage Direction of David Belasco*, pp. 41-46.

16 *New York Times*, January 31, 1904.

17 Winter, *Life*, I, p. 95.

18 *Ibid.*, I, p. 95. Katherine Goodale, *Behind the Scenes with Edwin Booth* (Boston, 1931) and Charles Townsend Copeland, *Edwin Booth* (Boston, 1901) both describe Booth's rehearsal technique, or lack of it.

19 Winter, I, p. 109.

20 Henri Nathansen, *William Bloch* (Copenhagen, 1928), p. 46.

21 William Winter, *Other Days* (New York, 1908), p. 325.

22 *Ibid.*, pp. 322-323. Meyerhold's antinaturalistic conviction that "the actor is the most important element on a stage" and that when "the naturalistic director made the ensembles more

important . . . the work of the actors became passive" and less effective makes for an interesting comparison with Winter's earlier view. See *Directors on Directing*, p. 168.

23 Robert Edmond Jones, *The Dramatic Imagination* (New York, 1941), pp. 37-38.

24 Belasco, *Stage Door*, pp. 120-121.

25 Stanislavski, p. 525.

26 Winter, *Life*, I, p. 264. *Plays Produced under the Stage Direction of David Belasco*, pp. 6-19, lists 235 titles.

27 Quoted in Craig Timberlake, *The Life and Work of David Belasco, The Bishop of Broadway* (New York, 1954), pp. 62-63.

28 Quoted from Belasco, "My Life's Story," *Hearst's Magazine*, in Winter, *Life*, I, p. 57.

29 Arthur Hornblow, *A History of the Theatre in America* (New York, 1965), II, p. 206.

30 Cf. Richard Moody, *America Takes the Stage* (Bloomington, 1955), pp. 28-29.

31 Winter, *Life*, I, pp. 97-98.

32 *Ibid.*, I, p. 99.

33 *Ibid.*, I, p. 99.

34 Belasco, *Stage Door*, p. 163.

35 Winter, *Life*, I, p. 108.

36 *Hearst's Magazine* XXVI (1914), 350; quoted in Timberlake, p. 65.

37 Winter, *Life*, I, p. 115.

38 Hornblow, II, pp. 315-316; see also Timberlake, pp. 67-82.

39 *Hearst's Magazine* XXVI, 610; Hornblow, II, p. 316.

40 Winter, *Life*, I, p. 256.

41 Quoted in Gorelik, p. 160.

42 Winter, *Life*, I, pp. 187-188.

43 *Ibid.*, I, p. 186.

44 *Ibid.*, I, pp. 113-114. The play was presented at the San Francisco Grand Opera House, rented by Maguire for the occasion.

45 *Ibid.*, I, p. 202.

46 For more about Belasco's unusual personality, see, for exam-

ple, Montrose J. Moses, "David Belasco, The Astonishing Versatility of a Veteran Producer," *Theatre Guild Magazine* VII (November 1929), 29.

47 Winter, *Life*, I, p. 264.

## CHAPTER TWO

1 Winter, *Life*, I, pp. 293-294.

2 For an excellent description of this theatre, see *The Scientific American*, April 5, 1884.

3 For an illustrated account of Booth's Theatre, see "Booth's Theatre, Behind the Scenes," *Appleton's Journal* (1870).

4 Barnard Hewitt, *Theatre U.S.A. 1668-1957* (New York, 1959), p. 253. For additional information, see Oral Sumner Coad and Edwin Mims, Jr., *The American Stage*, The Pageant of America XIV (New Haven, 1929), p. 268.

5 *New York Morning Telegraph*, August 9, 1925; quoted in *"Deburau" by Sacha Guitry, as Produced by David Belasco* (New York, 1925), p. 178.

6 An interesting description of the decoration and appearance of the auditorium in the Belasco-Stuyvesant is provided by a small booklet, anonymous and unpaged, *The First Night in David Belasco's Stuyvesant Theatre* (New York Public Library Theatre Collection, MCMVII). More recently, "Attending the Theatre in 1902," in Garff B. Wilson's *Three Hundred Years of American Drama and Theatre* (Englewood Cliffs, N.J., 1973), pp. 287-296, attempts an impressionistic description of the opening of the first Belasco Theatre.

7 Winter, *Life*, II, pp. 56-57 and 239-240.

8 Belasco, *Stage Door*, pp. 163-164.

9 Winter, *Life*, I, p. 109.

10 Belasco, *Stage Door*, p. 164.

11 In Moses and Brown, p. 234.

12 *The New Republic*, February 28, 1923; quoted in Hewitt, pp. 349-350.

13 Quoted in Coad and Mims, p. 241.

14 *May Blossom* was published in a Samuel French edition in 1884.

15 These plays are published in *The Plays of Henry C. De Mille Written in Collaboration with David Belasco,* ed. Robert Hamilton Ball, in America's Lost Plays XVII (Princeton, 1941).

16 Quoted in Montrose J. Moses, *The American Dramatist* (Boston, 1925), p. 240.

## CHAPTER THREE

1 David Belasco, "Stage Realism of the Future," *Theatre Magazine* (September 1913), 90.

2 "David Belasco Tells Alan Dale," *New York Journal,* December 8, 1901.

3 *Theatre Magazine* (September 1913), 87.

4 "David Belasco" in *American Drama and Its Critics,* ed. Alan S. Downer (Toronto and Chicago, 1965), pp. 37-38.

5 *New York Herald,* December 14, 1902.

6 George Pierce Baker, *Dramatic Technique* (Boston, 1919), p. 21.

7 *Brooklyn Times,* October 8, 1903.

8 Cf. Alan S. Downer, *Fifty Years of American Drama, 1900-1950* (Chicago, 1966), p. 39.

9 The majority of the Belasco plays mentioned here are contained either in David Belasco, *The Heart of Maryland and Other Plays,* ed. Glenn Hughes and George Savage, America's Lost Plays XVIII (Princeton, 1941), or David Belasco, *Six Plays* (Boston, 1929). For specific instances, however, see the Bibliography for this study.

10 George Jean Nathan, *The Critic and the Drama* (New York, 1922), p. 33.

11 *New York Herald Tribune,* May 15, 1931. That Belasco's popular plays thus reflect a sociological image of their time is an interesting subject in itself: cf. H. L. Kleinfeld, "The Theatrical Career of David Belasco," unpublished dissertation (Harvard, 1956).

12 *The Illustrated American,* April 7, 1894; see also Timberlake, p. 220.

13 *Theatre Magazine* (September 1913), 87.

14 Shaw's review appears in *Our Theatres in the Nineties* (Lon-

don, 1932), III, pp. 358-361. His famous review of the Adelphi revival of *The Girl I Left behind Me* (*ibid.*, I, pp. 92-97) advances a similar type of argument.

15 *Philadelphia Record*, October 29, 1905.

16 Belasco, *Six Plays*, pp. vi-vii.

17 *New York Herald Tribune*, May 15, 1931.

18 The promptbook for this play, containing many notes and ground plans, is in the New York Public Library Theatre Collection (NCOF+). This stage direction is reprinted in Belasco, *The Heart of Maryland and Other Plays*, pp. 235-236.

19 None has described this tradition more vividly than M. Willson Disher: see *Melodrama, Plots That Thrilled* (London, 1954).

20 "David Belasco Attacks Stage Tradition," *Theatre Magazine* (May 1911), 166.

21 Winter, *Life*, I, p. 328.

22 See especially the *New York Times*, November 24, 1889.

23 Belasco, *Stage Door*, p. 46. *Ibid.*, pp. 41-53, presents a detailed description of his working methods in this respect. See also *The Plays of Henry C. De Mille Written in Collaboration with David Belasco*, pp. xii-xiii.

24 Belasco, *Stage Door*, p. 73.

25 *New York Journal*, December 8, 1901.

26 *American Drama and Its Critics*, p. 38.

27 Belasco, *Stage Door*, p. 52. The Samuel French edition, "set up from the acting prompt manuscript of the play," appeared in 1915.

28 Cf. Belasco, *Stage Door*, pp. 52-53.

29 *Ibid.*, p. 167; Winter, *Life*, II, pp. 454-455.

30 Belasco, *Stage Door*, p. 61.

31 "David Belasco Tells How He Develops Stars and Produces Plays," *New York Herald*, April 17, 1904.

32 James L. Ford, *The Story of Du Barry* (New York, 1902) and John Cecil Clay, *Mrs. Leslie Carter in David Belasco's Du Barry* (New York, 1902).

33 "Staging a Popular Restaurant," *Theatre Magazine* (October 1912), 104, x-xi.

34 *Ibid.*, 104.
35 The typed promptbook for this play is in the New York Public Library Theatre Collection (NCOF+).
36 Gorelik, p. 164.
37 William Winter, *The Wallet of Time* (New York, 1913), II, pp. 177-178.
38 *Saturday Evening Post*, January 15, 1908.
39 Arthur Ruhl, *Second Nights* (New York, 1944), p. 255.
40 "A Few Reflections—by David Belasco," *New York Herald*, December 14, 1902.
41 Promptbook contained in the New York Public Library Theatre Collection (NCOF+).
42 *New York Herald*, December 14, 1902.
43 From the promptbook for *The Charity Ball*, in brown covers, dated 1889, and containing a blueprint ground plan, in the New York Public Library Theatre Collection. Unfortunately this collection makes no cataloguing distinction between this copy and three other, inferior, promptbooks for the same play; all four are simply catalogued NCOF+, a method which can only be called capricious. The printed version of the play in *The Plays of Henry C. De Mille*, pp. 201-268, provides far less detailed directions and descriptions.
44 Nathansen, p. 75.
45 Clayton Hamilton, *The Theory of the Theatre* (New York, 1914), p. 14.
46 "Madame Butterfly's Cocoon," 179.
47 Samuel French edition, p. 10. See note 27 above.
48 *The American Stage of To-Day* (Boston, 1908), p. 210.
49 Belasco, *Stage Door*, p. 195.
50 Quoted in *Directors on Directing*, p. 136.
51 Winter, *Life*, I, p. 418.
52 Belasco, *Stage Door*, pp. 239-251.
53 David Belasco, "How I Stage My Plays," *Theatre Magazine* (December 1902), 31-32.
54 *Ibid.*, 32.
55 *New York Times*, October 23, 1938. Retold in Gorelik, pp. 171-172.

56 "How Belasco Creates Dramatic Stars," *Current Literature* (April 1907), 435, 438.

57 David Belasco, *Theatre Magazine* (September 1913), 87.

58 Belasco, *Stage Door*, p. 53.

59 Moses, *Theatre Guild Magazine* vii (November 1929), 30.

60 Vsevolod Meyerhold, "The Theater Theatrical," in *Directors on Directing*, pp. 164-168.

61 Belasco, *Stage Door*, pp. 56, 165.

62 Quoted in Lee Simonson, *The Stage Is Set* (New York, 1963), pp. 358, 370.

63 See Belasco, *Stage Door*, pp. 181-182, and his elaborate light plot in the production book published by Samuel French (New York, 1915).

64 "The Psychology of the Stage Switchboard," *Theatre Magazine* (August 1909), 65.

65 *New York Dramatic Mirror*, October 19, 1901.

66 Louis Hartmann, *Theatre Lighting: A Manual of the Stage Switchboard* (New York, 1930; rep. 1970), p. 26.

67 Winter, *Life*, ii, p. 247. Kenneth Macgowan observes that Belasco first used spots to follow the actors around the stage, unknown to the audience, in Avery Hopwood's *Nobody's Widow* in 1908-09. The promptbook, with position plans and other notes, is in the Museum of the City of New York (43.98.186).

68 Hamilton, pp. 190-191. Hartmann describes these effects in chapter 3, "A Ghost Comes In," pp. 32-41.

69 Jones, *The Dramatic Imagination*, pp. 112-113.

70 Tennessee Williams, *The Glass Menagerie* in *American Drama*, ed. Alan S. Downer (New York, 1960), pp. 223-224.

71 See Belasco, *Stage Door*, pp. 164, 175-176.

72 "Poetry in Light: A Prophecy for the Drama by Mr. Belasco," *New York Herald*, January 4, 1903.

73 The opera received its first U.S. production in New York in 1906; its most illustrious performance took place at the Metropolitan in 1907, starring Enrico Caruso as Lieutenant Pinkerton, Geraldine Farrar as Cho-Cho-San, and Louise Homer as Susuki.

74 This celebrated scene is described in Winter, *Life*, I, pp. 480-482, Gorelik, pp. 164-165, and by Montrose Moses in *Six Plays*, pp. 5-7.

75 Winter, *Life*, I, p. 481; the reviews of the production amply confirm this assertion.

76 "Poetry in Light," *New York Herald*, January 4, 1903.

77 Hamilton, p. 178.

78 Blanche Bates's copy, a typescript with notes and directions in ink, is in the Museum of the City of New York (43.98.180).

79 Belasco, *Stage Door*, pp. 177-180; Winter, *Life*, II, pp. 83-84.

80 Eaton, "Madame Butterfly's Cocoon," 178.

81 Belasco, *Six Plays*, p. 224.

82 Belasco, *Stage Door*, p. 179.

83 For accounts of Belasco's experiments, see *ibid.*, pp. 58-60, and Winter, *Life*, II, p. 84.

84 "Poetry in Light," *New York Herald*, January 4, 1903.

85 Hartmann, pp. 65-66. Cf. Arthur Hobson Quinn, *A History of American Drama from the Civil War to the Present Day* (New York, 1936), pp. 193-194; Winter, *Life*, II, pp. 245-246. James M. Feeney, "New Method of Stage Lighting," *Lighting Journal* (October 1915), 217-219, also provides an account of lighting in the Belasco Theatre.

86 Winter, *Life*, I, p. 354.

87 Quoted in *ibid.*, II, p. 247.

88 Kenneth Macgowan, *The Theatre of Tomorrow* (New York, 1922), pp. 51-52; Huneker, "David Belasco," pp. 35-36.

89 Belasco, *Stage Door*, p. 74.

90 Lloyd Morris, *Curtain Time* (New York, 1953), p. 296. See also "A Rehearsal under Belasco," *Theatre Magazine* (February 1905), 42-43.

91 Belasco, *Stage Door*, p. 75.

92 David Belasco, "About Acting," *The Saturday Evening Post*, September 24, 1921.

93 Cf. Garff B. Wilson, *A History of American Acting* (Bloomington, 1966), p. 205.

94 "How I Created 'Simon Levi,'" *The Theatre* I (March 1902), 17.

95 *My Life in Art*, p. 397.

96 Belasco, *Stage Door*, p. 72.

97 See Winter, *Life*, ii, p. 120.

98 George Arliss, *Up the Years from Bloomsbury* (Boston, 1927), p. 207.

99 "Stage Realism of the Future," *Theatre Magazine* (September 1913), 86.

100 "The Wizard of the Commonplace," *Munsey's Magazine* (January 1908). Robinson Locke Collection, New York Public Library.

101 Vladimir Nemirovitch-Danchenko, *My Life in the Russian Theatre* (New York, 1968), pp. 162-163. Cf. *My Life in Art*, p. 420.

102 "David Belasco Attacks Stage Tradition," *Theatre Magazine* (May 1911), 166.

103 Belasco, *Stage Door*, p. 169.

104 "About Acting," *Saturday Evening Post*, September 24, 1921.

105 David Belasco, "Why I Produce Unprofitable Plays," *Theatre Magazine* (March 1929), 22, 68.

106 Arliss, p. 207.

107 *Theatre Magazine* (May 1911), 168.

108 Belasco, *Stage Door,* p. 64.

109 Jones, p. 82.

110 Belasco, *Stage Door*, p. 237.

111 Jones, pp. 118-119.

112 Simonson, p. 373.

113 Jones, p. 26.

114 *Theatre Arts Anthology: A Record and a Prophecy* (New York, 1950), p. 386.

115 *Ibid.*, p. 397.

116 Belasco, *Stage Door*, pp. 241-242.

117 *Ibid.*, pp. 166-167.

## CHAPTER FOUR

1 Quoted in Timberlake, p. 225.

2 New York Public Library Theatre Collection (NCOF+), black covers. The play was never published. Most Belasco manu-

scripts contain the following notation: "Property of David Belasco, Belasco Theatre, NYC. This manuscript has been copied from the original prompt-book of the play, as produced under David Belasco's direct supervision. It is earnestly requested that it shall not be uselessly marked or otherwise defaced, as it is the desire of the Belasco Play Bureau to keep all manuscripts and parts in as perfect a condition as possible for the good of all." Dialogue and stage directions quoted in this chapter are from this manuscript.

3 See the letters to Egerton Castle from Belasco, August 29, 1904 and March 3, 1905, in Winter, *Life*, II, pp. 106, 108.
4 Belasco, *Stage Door*, p. 76.
5 Winter, *Life*, II, pp. 95-96.
6 In the New York *Staats Zeitung*, December 10, 1903. Robinson Locke Collection, New York Public Library.
7 Winter, *Life*, II, p. 97.
8 See Belasco, *Stage Door*, pp. 176-177, and *Six Plays*, pp. 7, 151.
9 Winter, *Life*, II, p. 101, makes the same observation, but adds the following, so typical of his nature: "Noiseless falls/ the foot of Time/ That only falls on flowers."
10 Gorelik, p. 494.
11 *Commercial Advertiser*, December 10, 1903.
12 Winter, *Life*, II, pp. 98-99.
13 *Ibid.*, II, p. 99.
14 *Ibid.*, II, pp. 99-100.

## CHAPTER FIVE

1 Belasco, *Six Plays*, p. 307.
2 Winter, *Life*, II, p. 205.
3 Belasco, *Six Plays*, p. 317.
4 David Belasco, *The Girl of the Golden West*, Samuel French edition (New York, 1915) was "set up from the acting prompt manuscript of the play" and represents the most reliable source of information about production details. Also utilized in this chapter is Blanche Bates's acting manuscript, preserved in the Museum of the City of New York (43.98.184)

and containing several directions for effects that Belasco seems subsequently to have altered in practice.

5 See, for example, Moody, pp. 19-20.

6 Gorelik, p. 165.

7 Winter, *Life*, I, p. 257.

8 See Disher, *Melodrama, Plots That Thrilled*, pp. 10, 18.

9 Winter, *Life*, II, p. 205. To lose sight of this seriously intended purpose is to invite disaster in performing the play; hence when a rare professional production of it by Theatre-on-the-Green, Wellesley, Mass., opened at the Phyllis Anderson Theatre in New York in 1957, the *World Telegram and Sun* (October 7, 1957) advised patrons to "go prepared to laugh," and the send-up closed in five days.

10 Ruhl, *Second Nights*, pp. 247-248.

11 Winter, *Life*, I, p. 75.

12 See also A. Nicholas Vardac, *Stage to Screen: Theatrical Method from Garrick to Griffith* (New York, 1969), p. 113. Blanche Bates's script, with some blocking, is in the Museum of the City of New York (43.98.182).

13 Winter, *Life*, II, pp. 206-207.

14 Ruhl, pp. 248-249.

15 *Ibid.*, p. 248.

16 Belasco, *Stage Door*, p. 103.

17 "New York Acclaims Puccini's New Opera," *Theatre Magazine* (January 1911), 4. On the composer's enthusiastic acclaim of Belasco's contribution, see George Marek, *Puccini* (New York, 1951), p. 263.

18 Belasco, *Stage Door*, pp. 56-57, where the sunrise is, incidentally, incorrectly called a sunset.

## CHAPTER SIX

1 *New York Tribune*, January 20, 1909; see also Winter, *Life*, II, pp. 267-269.

2 Walter Prichard Eaton, *At the New Theatre and Others* (Boston, 1910), pp. 93-94.

3 *Theatre Magazine* (March 1909), 81.

4 Montrose J. Moses, ed., *Representative Plays by American Dramatists* (New York, 1921), III, p. 707.

5 *Theatre Magazine* (March 1909), 84.

6 Winter, *Life*, II, p. 270.

7 The promptbook, typewritten with handwritten notes and plans, is in the New York Public Library Theatre Collection (NCOF+). The printed version of this promptbook appears in Moses, *Representative Plays*, III, pp. 711-814.

8 Moses, III, pp. 715-716.

9 Belasco, *Stage Door*, p. 110.

10 Ward Morehouse, *Matinee Tomorrow* (New York, 1949), pp. 90, 91.

11 Promptbook manuscript in the New York Public Library Theatre Collection (NCOF+).

12 Belasco, *Stage Door*, p. 77.

13 Moses, III, pp. 445-448.

14 Winter, *Life*, II, p. 270.

15 Downer, *Fifty Years*, p. 33.

16 *Theatre Magazine* (May 1911), 168.

17 Quoted in Moses, III, p. 821.

18 *Ibid.*, p. 707.

19 Winter, *Life*, II, p. 270.

20 *Theatre Magazine* (March 1909), 81.

21 Eaton, *At the New Theatre*, pp. 96-97.

22 See also Lloyd Morris, "He Built a Theatre, Stars, and a Legend," *Theatre Arts* XXXVII (November 1953), 32.

23 Sayler, *Our American Theatre*, p. 53.

24 *New York Times*, September 7, 1931.


## CHAPTER SEVEN

1 A slightly altered version of this chapter was published in *Theatre Research* X (1969), 17-32.

2 David Magarschack, *Stanislavsky* (New York, 1951), p. 366.

3 *The Merchant of Venice: A Comedy by William Shakespeare, as Arranged for the Contemporary Stage by David Belasco* (New York, 1922) and *A Souvenir of Shakespeare's*

*The Merchant of Venice as Presented by David Belasco* (New York, 1923).

4 *Souvenir*, p. 10.

5 *Ibid.*, p. 12.

6 *Ibid.*, pp. 12-13.

7 *Immortal Shadows*, p. 43.

8 *Souvenir*, p. 21.

9 Jones, pp. 82, 26.

10 *Souvenir*, p. 18.

11 *Ibid.*, p. 31.

12 *Ibid.*, p. 32.

13 *Ibid.*, p. 32.

14 *Ibid.*, pp. 19-20.

15 All reviews dated December 22, 1922.

16 Cf. George C. D. Odell, *Shakespeare from Betterton to Irving* (London, 1920), II, p. 353.

17 Cf. *ibid.*, II, p. 423, and William Winter, *Shakespeare on the Stage*, First Series (New York, 1911), p. 176.

18 *Immortal Shadows*, p. 43.

19 Cf. *Stanislavski Produces Othello*, trans. Helen Novak (New York, 1948), pp. 108-109.

20 Cf. Arthur Colby Sprague, *Shakespeare and the Actors* (New York, 1963), p. 19.

21 Belasco, *Stage Door*, p. 229.

22 Cf. Sprague, p. 22.

23 Cf. Winter, *Shakespeare on the Stage*, pp. 176-177.

24 Sprague, p. 23.

25 Winter, *Shakespeare*, p. 177.

26 Cf. Odell, II, p. 403.

27 Cf. Winter, *Shakespeare*, p. 155.

28 *New York Times*, December 22, 1922.

29 *Souvenir*, p. 35. Belasco's didactic footnote in the printed promptbook (p. 150) is comparable: "Students of this play should note that *Shylock* does not use the word 'justice.' That is *Portia's* word. *Shylock* takes his stand upon *law* and demands *judgment*, according to law.—D.B."

30 Cf. Sprague, p. 28.

31 *Immortal Shadows*, p. 42.
32 See Winter, *Life*, ii, pp. 443-444.

## EPILOGUE

1 Guest reviewer for the *New York World*, December 14, 1928.
2 Hence one is disappointed to encounter in Travis Bogard's *Contour in Time: The Plays of Eugene O'Neill* (Oxford, 1972) an emotional and uncritical generalization such as the following: "In the main, however, Belasco's imitation of surface appearances was slavish and dull, a trivial naturalism whose product was without truth or delight" (p. 252).
3 Moses, p. 256.
4 The typed letter is in the Theatre Collection of the New York Public Library.
5 Belasco, *Stage Door*, pp. 219-220.
6 "The Theatre—Art and Instinct," in Oliver M. Sayler's *Revolt in the Arts* (New York, 1930), p. 190.
7 Eaton, "Madam Butterfly's Cocoon," 180.
8 Typed promptbook in the New York Public Library Theatre Collection (NCOF+), 1931. Never produced, this play bears no relation to Robert Buckner's screenplay "Virginia City," filmed by Warner Bros. in 1940.
9 David Belasco, "Why I Believe in the Little Things," *Ladies' Home Journal* (September 1911), 73.
10 Harold Clurman, *The Fervent Years* (New York, 1957), pp. 23, xii.
11 Eaton, 182.

# Chronology

## New York Productions of David Belasco's Major Plays and Adaptations

| | | |
|---|---|---|
| *La Belle Russe* | May  8, 1882 | (Adaptation of *Forget-Me-Not* by Herman Merivale and Charles Groves, and *The New Magdalen* by Wilkie Collins) |
| *The Stranglers of Paris* | Nov. 12, 1883 | (Dramatization of *Les Etrangleurs de Paris* by Adolphe Belot) |
| *May Blossom* | Apr. 12, 1884 | |
| *Valerie* | Feb. 15, 1886 | (Adaptation of *Fernande* by Victorien Sardou) |
| *The Highest Bidder* | May  3, 1887 | (Adaptation of *Trade* by J. M. Morton and R. Reece) |
| *Baron Rudolph* | Oct. 24, 1887 | (With Bronson Howard) |
| *The Wife* | Nov. 1, 1887 | (With Henry C. De Mille) |
| *Lord Chumley* | Aug. 20, 1888 | (With Henry C. De Mille) |
| *The Charity Ball* | Nov. 19, 1889 | (With Henry C. De Mille) |

| | | |
|---|---|---|
| *Men and Women* | Oct. 21, 1890 | (With Henry C. De Mille) |
| *Miss Helyett* | Nov. 3, 1891 | (Adaptation from the French of Maxime Boucheron) |
| *The Girl I Left behind Me* | Jan. 25, 1893 | (With Franklyn Fyles) |
| *The Younger Son* | Oct. 24, 1893 | (Adaptation of *Schlimme Saat* by O. Vischer) |
| *The Heart of Maryland* | Oct. 22, 1895 | |
| *Zaza* | Jan. 9, 1899 | (Adaptation from the French of Pierre Berton and Charles Simon) |
| *Naughty Anthony* | Jan. 8, 1900 | |
| *Madame Butterfly* | Mar. 5, 1900 | (Dramatization of the story by John Luther Long) |
| *Du Barry* | Dec. 25, 1901 | |
| *The Darling of the Gods* | Dec. 3, 1902 | (With John Luther Long) |
| *Sweet Kitty Bellairs* | Dec. 9, 1903 | (Dramatization of *The Bath Comedy* by Egerton and Agnes Castle) |
| *Adrea* | Jan. 11, 1905 | (With John Luther Long) |
| *The Girl of the Golden West* | Nov. 14, 1905 | |
| *The Rose of the Rancho* | Nov. 27, 1906 | (With R. W. Tully) |
| *A Grand Army Man* | Oct. 16, 1907 | (With Pauline Phelps and Marion Short) |
| *The Lily* | Dec. 23, 1909 | (Adapted from *Le Lys* by Pierre Wolff and Gaston Leroux) |
| *The Return of Peter Grimm* | Oct. 17, 1911 | |

227

| | | |
|---|---|---|
| *The Governor's Lady* | Sept. 9, 1912 | (With Alice Bradley) |
| *The Secret* | Dec. 23, 1913 | (Adaptation from the French of Henri Bernstein) |
| *The Son Daughter* | Nov. 19, 1919 | (With George Scarborough) |
| *Kiki* | Nov. 29, 1921 | (Adaptation from the French of André Picard) |
| *The Comedian* | Mar. 13, 1923 | (Adaptation from the French of Sacha Guitry) |
| *Laugh, Clown, Laugh* | Nov. 28, 1923 | (Adaptation with Tom Cushing of *Ridi Pagliaccio* by Fausto Martini) |
| *Fanny* | Sept. 21, 1926 | (With Willard Mack) |
| *Mima* | Dec. 12, 1928 | (Adaptation of *The Red Mill* by Ferenc Molnar) |

# Bibliography

Albert, Dora. "A Power in the Theatre at Seventy-five," *Forecast* xxxvi (Nov. 1929), 315-324.

Anderson, John. *The American Theatre.* New York, 1938.

Antoine, André. *Mes Souvenirs sur le Théâtre-Libre.* Paris, 1921.

Appia, Adolphe. *La Mise-en-scène du drame Wagnérien.* Paris, 1895.

———. *Die Musik und die Inszenierung.* Munich, 1899.

Arliss, George. *Up the Years from Bloomsbury.* Boston, 1927.

Baker, George Pierce. *Dramatic Technique.* Boston, 1919.

Belasco, David. "About Acting," *The Saturday Evening Post* (Sept. 24, 1921).

———. "David Belasco Attacks Stage Tradition," *Theatre Magazine* (May 1911), 164-168.

———. *The Girl of the Golden West.* New York: Samuel French, 1915.

———. *The Heart of Maryland and Other Plays,* eds. Glenn Hughes and George Savage. America's Lost Plays xviii. Princeton, 1941 (contains: *La Belle Russe,*

*The Stranglers of Paris, The Girl I Left behind Me, The Heart of Maryland*, and *Naughty Anthony*).

———. "How I Stage My Plays," *Theatre Magazine* (Dec. 1902), 31-32.

———. *May Blossom*. New York: Samuel French, 1884.

———. "My Life's Story," *Hearst's Magazine* xxv-xxvi (Mar. 1914-Dec. 1915).

———. *The Return of Peter Grimm*. New York: Samuel French, 1915.

———. *The Rose of the Rancho*. New York: Samuel French, 1915.

———. *Six Plays*. Boston, 1929 (contains: *Madame Butterfly, Du Barry, The Darling of the Gods, Adrea, The Girl of the Golden West*, and *The Return of Peter Grimm*).

———. "Stage Realism of the Future," *Theatre Magazine* (Sept. 1913), 86-90, ix.

———. *The Theatre through Its Stage Door*, ed. Louis V. Defoe. New York, 1919.

———. "Why I Produce Unprofitable Plays," *Theatre Magazine* (Mar. 1929), 22, 68.

Bentley, Eric, ed. *The Theory of the Modern Stage*. Penguin Books, 1968.

Bergman, Gösta M. *Den Moderna Teaterns Genombrott, 1890-1925*. Stockholm, 1966.

Bernheim, Alfred L. *The Business of the Theatre*. New York, 1932.

Blake, Ben. *The Awakening of the American Theatre*. New York, 1935.

Bogard, Travis. *Contour in Time: The Plays of Eugene O'Neill*. Oxford, 1972.

*Booth's Theatre, Behind the Scenes* (reprint from *Appleton's Journal*). New York, 1870.

Brown, John Mason. *Upstage: The American Theatre in Performance*. Cincinnati, 1916.

Brown, T. Allston. *A History of the New York Stage from . . . 1732 to 1901*. 3 vols. New York, 1903.

Clapp, Henry Austin. *Reminiscences of a Dramatic Critic*. Boston, 1902.

Clay, John Cecil. *Mrs. Leslie Carter in David Belasco's Du Barry*. New York, 1902.

Clurman, Harold. *The Fervent Years*. New York, 1957.

Coad, Oral Sumner and Edwin Mims, Jr. *The American Stage*. The Pageant of America xiv. New Haven, 1929.

Cole, Toby. *Acting, A Handbook of the Stanislavski Method*. New York, 1955.

Cole, Toby and H. K. Chinoy, eds. *Actors on Acting*. New York, 1954.

——. *Directors on Directing*. Indianapolis, 1963.

Copeland, Charles Townsend. *Edwin Booth*. Boston, 1901.

*"Deburau" by Sacha Guitry, as Produced by David Belasco*. New York, 1925.

[De Mille, Henry C.] *The Plays of Henry C. De Mille Written in Collaboration with David Belasco,* ed. Robert Hamilton Ball. America's Lost Plays xvii. Princeton, 1941 (contains: *The Wife, Lord Chumley, The Charity Ball,* and *Men and Women*).

Disher, M. Willson. *Melodrama, Plots That Thrilled*. London, 1954.

Downer, Alan S. *American Drama*. New York, 1960.

——, ed. *American Drama and Its Critics*. Toronto and Chicago, 1965.

Downer, Alan S. *Fifty Years of American Drama, 1900-1950*. Chicago, 1966.

Dransfield, Jane. "Behind the Scenes with Belasco," *Theatre Magazine* (Apr. 1922), 228-230, 260.

Duerr, Edwin. *The Length and Depth of Acting*. New York, 1963.

Eaton, Walter Prichard. *At the New Theatre and Others*. Boston, 1910.

———. "Madame Butterfly's Cocoon: A Sketch of David Belasco," *The American Scholar* v (Spring 1936), 172-182.

———. *Plays and Players*. Cincinnati, 1916.

*The First Night in David Belasco's Stuyvesant Theatre*. New York, n.d.

Ford, James L. *The Story of Du Barry*. New York, 1902.

Frohman, Daniel. *Daniel Frohman Presents: An Autobiography*. New York, 1935.

———. *Encore*. New York, 1937.

———. *Memories of a Manager*. New York, 1911.

Gagey, Edmond M. *Revolution in American Drama*. New York, 1947.

———. *The San Francisco Stage*. New York, 1950.

Gaige, Crosby. *Footlights and Highlights*. New York, 1948.

Gassner, John. *Directions in Modern Theatre and Drama*. New York, 1966.

Gelb, Arthur and Barbara. *O'Neill*. New York, 1962.

Goodale, Katherine. *Behind the Scenes with Edwin Booth*. Boston, 1931.

Gorelik, Mordecai. *New Theatres for Old*. New York, 1940.

Hamilton, Clayton. *The Theory of the Theatre*. New York, 1914.

Hapgood, Norman. *The Stage in America, 1897-1900*. New York, 1901.

Hartmann, Louis. *Theatre Lighting, A Manual of the Stage Switchboard*. London and New York, 1930.

Herne, James A. *Plays*, ed. Arthur Hobson Quinn. America's Lost Plays VII. Princeton, 1940.

Hewitt, Barnard. *Theatre U.S.A. 1668 to 1957*. New York, 1959.

*Historical and Romantic Plays,* ed. J. B. Russak. America's Lost Plays XVI. Princeton, 1941.

Hopkins, Arthur. *How's Your Second Act?* New York, 1918.

Hornblow, Arthur. *A History of the Theatre in America*. 2 vols. New York, 1965.

Hughes, Glenn. *A History of the American Theatre 1700-1950*. New York, 1951.

Huneker, James G. "David Belasco," *The Outlook* (Mar. 16, 1921), 418-422.

Jones, Robert Edmond. *The Dramatic Imagination*. New York, 1941.

Kleinfield, Herbert Leo. "The Theatrical Career of David Belasco," unpublished dissertation. Harvard, 1956.

Krow, Arthur Edwin. *Play Production in America*. New York, 1916.

Krutch, Joseph Wood. *The American Drama since 1918*. New York, 1957.

Laver, James. *Drama, Its Costume and Decor*. London, 1952.

Long, John Luther. "Madame Butterfly," *Century Magazine*, LV (1898), 374-392.

Long, John Luther. "William Winter's *Life of Belasco*," *Nation*, CVII (1918), 806.

Macgowan, Kenneth. *The Theatre of Tomorrow*. New York, 1921.

MacKaye, Percy. *Epoch: The Life of Steele MacKaye*. 2 vols. New York, 1927.

MacMinn, George R. *The Theatre of the Golden Era in California*. Caldwell, Idaho, 1941.

Magarshack, David. *Stanislavsky*. New York, 1951.

Marcosson, Isaac F. and Daniel Frohman. *Charles Frohman: Manager and Man*. New York, 1916.

Marek, George. *Puccini*. New York, 1951.

Marker, Frederick J. *Hans Christian Andersen and the Romantic Theatre*. Toronto and Oxford, 1971.

Marker, Lise-Lone. "Naturalismen i amerikansk teater: David Belasco," *Teatervidenskabelige studier*, ed. S. Christiansen. Copenhagen, 1969, pp. 108-135.

————. "Shakespeare and Naturalism: David Belasco Produces *The Merchant of Venice*," *Theatre Research* X (1969), 17-32.

Matthews, Brander. *Rip Van Winkle Goes to the Play*. New York, 1926.

*The Merchant of Venice: A Comedy by William Shakespeare, as Arranged for the Contemporary Stage by David Belasco*. New York, 1922.

Middleton, George. *These Things are Mine*. New York, 1947.

Mielziner, Jo. *Designing for the Theatre*. New York, 1965.

Moody, Richard. *America Takes the Stage*. Bloomington, 1955.

Morehouse, Ward. *Matinee Tomorrow*. New York, 1949.

Morris, Lloyd. *Curtain Time*. New York, 1953.

Moses, Montrose J. *The American Dramatist*. Boston, 1925.

———. "The Astonishing Versatility of a Veteran Producer," *Theatre Guild Magazine* VII (Nov. 1929), 27-30, 51.

———. "Belasco: Stage Realist," *Theatre Magazine* (May 1916), 336-337.

———, ed. *Representative Plays by American Dramatists*. 3 vols. New York, 1921.

Moses, Montrose J. and John Mason Brown, eds. *The American Theatre as Seen by Its Critics*. New York, 1934.

Nagler, A. M. *Sources of Theatrical History*. New York, 1952.

Nathan, George Jean. *The Critic and the Drama*. New York, 1922.

———. *Mr. George Jean Nathan Presents*. New York, 1917.

———. *The Theatre, the Drama, the Girls*. New York, 1921.

Nathansen, Henri. *William Bloch*. Copenhagen, 1928.

Nemirovitch-Danchenko, Vladimir. *My Life in the Russian Theatre*. Boston, 1936.

Odell, George C. D. *Annals of the New York Stage* XI-XV. New York, 1939-49.

———. *Shakespeare from Betterton to Irving*. 2 vols. London, 1920.

*Plays Produced under the Stage Direction of David Belasco*. New York, 1925.

Quinn, Arthur Hobson. *A History of the American Drama from the Civil War to the Present Day*. New York, 1936.

*The Return of Peter Grimm, Novelized from the Play by David Belasco*. New York, 1912.

Ruhl, Arthur. *Second Nights*. New York, 1914.

Sayler, Oliver M. *Our American Theatre*. New York, 1923.

———. *Revolt in the Arts*. New York, 1930.

Shaw, George Bernard. *Our Theatres in the Nineties*. 3 vols. London, 1932.

Simonson, Lee. *The Stage Is Set*. New York, 1963.

Southern, Richard. *Changeable Scenery*. London, 1952.

*A Souvenir of Shakespeare's The Merchant of Venice, as Presented by David Belasco*. New York, 1923.

Sprague, Arthur Colby. *Shakespeare and the Actors*. New York, 1963.

Stanislavski, Constantin. *An Actor Prepares*. London, 1959.

———. *My Life in Art*. New York, 1956.

*Stanislavski Produces Othello,* trans. Helen Novak. New York, 1948.

Starr, Frances. "How I Prepare a Role," *The Delineator* xcvi (June 1920), 23, 96-97.

———. "My Stage Principles," *Forum* lxi (Mar. 1919), 335-342.

*Theatre Arts Anthology: A Record and a Prophecy*. New York, 1950.

Timberlake, Craig. *The Life and Work of David Belasco, the Bishop of Broadway*. New York, 1954.

Towse, John Ranken. *Sixty Years in the Theatre*. New York, 1916.

Vardac, A. Nicholas. *Stage to Screen: Theatrical Method from Garrick to Griffith*. New York, 1969.

Warfield, David. "How I Created 'Simon Levi,'" *The Theatre* 1 (Mar. 1902), 16-17.

Wiingaard, Jytte. *William Bloch og Holberg*. Copenhagen, 1966.

Wilson, Garff B. *A History of American Acting*. Bloomington, 1966.

———. *Three Hundred Years of American Drama and Theatre*. Englewood Cliffs, N.J., 1973.

Winter, William. *The Life of David Belasco*. 2 vols. New York, 1918.

———. *Other Days*. New York, 1908.

———. *Shakespeare on the Stage*, First Series. New York, 1911.

———. *Vagrant Memories*. New York, 1915.

———. *The Wallet of Time*. 2 vols. New York, 1913.

Woollcott, Alexander. *Enchanted Aisles*. New York, 1924.

———. *The Letters of Alexander Woollcott*. New York, 1944.

———. *Mrs. Fiske, Her Views on Actors, Acting, and the Problems of Production*. New York, 1917.

Young, Stark. *Immortal Shadows*. New York, 1948.

Zola, Émile. *Le Naturalisme au théâtre*. Paris, 1881.


*Newspapers and Periodicals:*

*American Magazine*
*The American Scholar*
*Appleton's Journal*
*Brooklyn Times*
*The Century Magazine*

*The Commercial Advertiser*
*Current Literature*
*Harper's Weekly*
*Hearst's Magazine*
*The Illustrated American*
*Munsey's Magazine*
*The New Republic*
*New York American*
*New York Evening Mail*
*New York Evening Telegram*
*New York Evening World*
*New York Herald*
*New York Herald Tribune*
*New York Journal*
*New York Morning Telegraph*
*New York Sun*
*New York Times*
*New York Tribune*
*New York World Telegram and Sun*
*Philadelphia Record*
*Saturday Evening Post*
*The Smart Set*
*The Theatre*
*Theatre Arts Magazine*
*Theatre Guild Magazine*
*Theatre Magazine*

# Index

239

*Library of Congress Cataloging in Publication Data*

Marker, Lise-Lone
David Belasco; naturalism in the American theatre.

Bibliography: p.
1. Belasco, David, 1853-1931.
PN2287.B4M37     792'.0233'0924     74-2970
ISBN 0-691-04626-3